CAMPFIRE
SMOKE
~ *and* ~
# TRAIL DUST

CAMPFIRE SMOKE
~ *and* ~
TRAIL DUST

TALES FROM A HIGH SIERRA PACK COOK

Irene Kritz

Aventine Press

Published by Aventine Press
55 East Emerson St.
Chula Vista CA, 91911
www.aventinepress.com

ISBN: 1-59330-804-3

Library of Congress Control Number: 2012922249
Library of Congress Cataloging-in-Publication Data
Campfire Smoke and Trail Dust/ Irene Kritz

Printed in the United States of America

Contents

INTRODUCTION

It's evening in the high lonesome of the Sierra Nevada Mountains. The dark shapes of the surrounding pine trees tower against a million blazing stars. The smell of wood smoke fills the air as firelight dances on the faces of the folks gathered around the campfire. This group includes packers, wranglers, the pack cook, and all the trail-weary guests. Entertaining the guests is an accepted part of the crew's job. So such an evening may include a packer playing guitar and singing campfire songs, a wrangler reciting cowboy poetry, someone warming up his harmonica, and as the evening winds down everyone telling stories and jokes.

The stocky old lady sitting in the dark is me, Irene, the pack cook. My work day started at 4 o'clock this morning when I started the kitchen fire and put on the coffee. After that I cooked breakfast, put out lunch makings, washed up the kitchen, tore down and packed up camp, rode 15 miles on mule back guiding the guests to the next camp, built a new camp, and fixed dinner. Now that the dishes are done, all I have left to do is the "entertain the guests" part of the job.

My campfire talents are pretty limited. In fact I have two jokes and one slightly off-color song that I know. So usually I just tell stories about the 40-some years I have spent working with various pack trains in the High Sierra. With a job that involves horses, mules, rocky cliffs, raging storms, roaring rivers, wild animals, and some really amazing people, there are lots of stories to tell. And "truth be told" I like to talk. Eventually, guests started coming up to me and saying that I should write some of these stories down and put them in a book.

Secretly, I was pretty flattered. So a few years back when I was too busted up to ride for a year or so, I amused myself by writing some of the stories down. These are those tales. Some of them are pretty good, though I do have a sneaking suspicion that the folks who told me to write actually just hoped I would quit talking so much.

FIRST WRANGLE

When a new cook first comes to work in the high lonesome, there's a whole heck of a lot to learn. You gotta learn to recognize good firewood, build fires, feed up to a hundred people, haul water, care for your fresh, guard your supplies from bears, and listen to a lot of lies around the campfire. You also need to know the trails, the country and the stock because you're responsible for the guests whenever you're riding from camp to camp.

Back in '64 when I was green as grass I sorta stumbled into a job with Mt. Whitney Pack Trains. After spending most of my first summer back at the pack station, I finally made my first big trip in the high country. We had about 35 people, which was what a big trip looked like in those days. We were doing a ten day loop from Carroll Creek to Whitney Portals. On our first day we rode from the floor of the Owens Valley up to Overhaulser Meadow on Little Cottonwood Creek. Our second move was over New Army Pass to Rock Creek where we camped at Nathan Meadow. I was learning a lot in my new job. I could haul water from the creek, peel potatoes and carrots by the dozens, and wash pots, pans and big metal plates by the hour. Since I didn't know the country, when I rode with the guests I mostly learned to eat dust while riding drag.

That next day at Nathan Meadow, we were all up way before dawn. Tommy Jefferson, our Mono-Paiute-Shoshone boss, always started the fires before first light so he could have coffee before anyone headed out to wrangle. Tommy's wife, Barbara, was cooking this part of the trip and told Tommy that she didn't need me for that breakfast. So he decided that it was a good opportunity for me to learn to wrangle.

Later on I learned that different outfits have different ways of wrangling the stock. At this time I firmly believed that the way things were done at Mt. Whitney was the only way. Mt. Whitney Pack Trains packers turned all the stock out to graze for the night. At very first light before the animals started to move, each packer who was wrangling that day took a nosebag with a little grain and a bridle. They then set out walking and looking for the stock which at times could be as much as 20 miles away. Each wrangler would set out cutting for tracks until he found some stock. When he found the first animals, he would catch and bridle a riding horse and swing up bareback. From there he would ride until he located the rest of the animals and then drive them back to camp.

Rock Creek is in a long, narrow canyon so most times you only need two wranglers; one to gather up canyon and one to go down. This day Stephanie was going to go up and Eric was supposed to wrangle down. Tommy sent me with Stephanie to learn how the cow ate the cabbage. Stephanie was the friend from school who had gotten me this job, so I knew she knew what to do and I hoped she would look out for me. With each of us carrying our nosebags and bridles, we headed out up canyon looking for 60 head of loose horses and mules. A few miles out we found our first animals, caught two, and got mounted. Now I was kind of a timid rider and I sure hoped this bareback riding would be limited to a sedate walk. We got to a place where we could cut for tracks all the way across the canyon. There were no tracks so we knew there were no animals above us in the canyon.

Then we started down pushing the stock we had found on the way. We had about 20 head. It was a fine cold morning and the sedate walk rapidly escalated into a wild gallop down through the boulders and back to camp. I couldn't believe I was still up on the horse when we arrived in camp. I guess I was just too scared of all those rocks to fall off.

We were catching up the stock when Tommy came by mumbling that that darn Eric was still in his bedroll. Being grateful that I had survived the wild ride down the canyon, I felt sorry for anyone who had to go down canyon and find the other 40 head. Right at that moment Tommy came up with the brilliant idea that more wrangling would be just the thing for the new girl. One good thing was that I had time enough to saddle before we pulled out. I was pretty thrilled to not be bareback any more. I was also at least a little thrilled to be riding out with Eric. Tall and blond with almond shaped blue eyes, he was about as purty as a guy could get. I was new and green and thought sure he must be a real cowboy. Later I figured out that some guys are hands and some guys are more like feet. Eric was definitely a foot. While Eric was saddling, Tommy gave us a little advice about wrangling lower Rock Creek. It seemed like once you got below the crossing there were lots of places where you could sink your horse in a bog, and if you went too far down canyon, the floor of the canyon would just disappear in a thousand foot drop into Kern Canyon. Just thinking about riding through that made my mouth go dry.

Oh, well, since I had no idea what to do, I just figured I could follow Eric and everything would be OK. Starting out down canyon, that's exactly what I did, followed Eric. There must have been fresh tracks on the trail because Eric never left that trail clear down to the crossing.

At one place I pointed out a set of tracks that cut across the canyon. Eric looked at me like something he'd found on the bottom of his boot and said, "Never follow a single set of tracks!" My delicate, girlish feelings stung by this rebuke, I rode on in silence. After a while I tried to ask him another question. He whirled around and hissed, "Never talk to me when I'm tracking." Being as we were riding straight down a Park Service trail, that seemed a little extreme, but I shut up anyway.

After we got to the place where the trail crossed the stream and left the canyon, we were on our own. Eric told me to cross the stream and check the north side of the creek for tracks. Now I was all alone. It was foggy and the visibility wasn't good. Every green patch of ground seemed to be a bog. I hadn't been in the Sierra long enough to recognize that change in the green of a meadow that tells you not to step there. After reaching a point on that side of the creek that was impassable and still not finding any horse sign, I worked my way back up to the crossing. The stock had to be down the south side of the creek where Eric had gone. I figured that I would just catch up with him and then I wouldn't drown in a bog or get lost in the fog. The farther down I went, the more trouble I seemed to be in. You couldn't see much through the fog and everywhere your horse stepped seemed to be one more bog. At this point I just wanted to go back to camp. I would have done it, but I couldn't face the ridicule that I would receive if I turned yellow.

Right at that moment I spotted a single set of tracks crossing the meadow toward an island of pines on the far side. I didn't care that it was only one set. If I could find a single animal I would have an excuse to take it back to camp. As I worked my way across the meadow toward the trees, to my unbelieving ears came the joyous sound of a bell. It was a bell mare and three mules. Now I could go back without looking like a complete idiot. As I waited for them to come across the open meadow and head up canyon, I realized there were more animals in those pines. As I watched in wonder, all 40 head of mules and horses strolled out of the trees and headed up canyon. They just lined out, walked to the trail and headed back to camp. I fell in line behind them trying to pretend like I was the last of the great wranglers. The rest of the way back to camp I entertained myself with visions of how impressed the packers would be when I came in with all 40 head all by myself.

Of course, they weren't all that impressed being as they did that kind of stuff all the time. In fact they sat there eating breakfast and let the stock go right on through camp and out the other side. I galloped around to cut them off and turned them back through camp. The guys let them go again. I turned them a second time and once more no one caught them, only this time the guys were laughing. They thought it was pretty funny watching the new kid running back and forth trying to keep 40 head of stock in camp while no one was catching up. Pretty damn embarrassed, I let the stock go, bailed off my horse, and told them they could get their own #?%* horses. Tommy came over and asked what I was so upset about. I started yelling about all the things that had happened that morning and somewhere in that tirade I included the part where Eric told me not to talk while he was tracking. Now if you know Tommy, you know he's a jokester. And when he gets something on you it is forever. Poor Eric, for the rest of the summer whenever he came to the campfire, Tommy would say, "Shhh, everyone be quiet. It's the silent tracker."

Eric never forgave me, but at least I learned a little bit about wrangling.

SLEEPIN' WARM

So it was starting to snow in Outpost Meadow. It was late August and the last night of a ten day trip. The weather had been warm and beautiful, but today as we climbed over Mt. Whitney the temperature started to drop. As we reached camp, the clouds were dropping down the peaks and the winds were singing in the canyons. Outpost Camp is a pocket in the rocks carved out by glacial action. The whole pocket is only about ten acres. The lower half is creek, willows and bogs. The upper half is a pleasant campsite on dry sand among sheltering pines. Just above camp is a magnificent waterfall tumbling off the sheer walls that surrounded us.

Being only my third year working the high country as a pack cook, I was still using whatever I could find for camp equipment. My saddle and riding gear were pretty good, but I was definitely lacking in the sleeping bag department. In fact my bag was one of those ten dollar, Dacron specials from Sears. Being a poverty stricken student the rest of the year, it was about the best I could do. After freezing every night for two years, I started looking for a way to improve my sleeping arrangements. If I hadn't been short, fat, and less than average looking, I might have tried for one of those tall, cute packer-type bed warmers, but no such luck. Besides, Whitney Pack Trains was a family outfit and they frowned on that sort of thing. Daydreaming aside, I actually found an abandoned sleeping bag in the old tack shed. The reason it had been abandoned was instantly obvious. It was exactly like the flimsy one I already had. Figuring that two flimsy bags might add up to at least a little warmth, I put them one inside the other. So those were my sleeping arrangements that night at Outpost.

We were a pretty big group, made up of 26 guests and a crew of about ten or twelve. Our boss, Tommy Jefferson, was head packer. His wife Barbara was head cook. There were four other packers, and Lynn and I were the kitchen crew. As always, the Jefferson's kids and neighbors made up the rest of the crew. After dinner that night, the entire group huddled around the campfire for the usual last night stories and jokes. Even with a roaring fire; the dropping temperatures, rising winds, and spitting snow sent most people to bed early. So Lynn and I were left at the fire trying to figure out the best way to survive the night. Lynn had a nice down bag, but it was cold enough that she was still worried. Crew never carried tents, so that wasn't an option. We discussed the theory that your day clothes always carried a thin layer of sweat that would chill you if you tried to sleep in them. We were young and foolish so it was decided that our girly little nighties would keep us warmer. We also borrowed two pack tarps each, one for over and one for under our beds. Nowadays pack tarps are plastic and sweat all over your bed, but in those days tarps were treated canvas and made a great bed cover. At some other outfits, we might have taken some mule pads or saddle blankets for added warmth. Since that could put dirt and folds in the blankets which would sore an animal's back, you didn't do that at Mt. Whitney unless you were looking to get fired.

Our last and most brilliant idea involved sleeping by the fire. Most everyone knows that sleeping too close to a fire is dangerous. Our plan involved sleeping about nine feet out from the fire and building a little rock wall by the foot of each of our bags to keep us from sliding too close to the flames. So we put all these plans into action and soon were snuggled down for the night. The last thing I did was to roll my corduroy coat up to use for a pillow.

In the wee hours of the morning, I came partially awake and realized that I was warm. How great! All our plans had worked and for the first time in my years in the Sierras, I was sleeping warm. Something hit my feet and someone was yelling. I kicked back at them and said, "Leave me alone, I'm sleepin' warm." Whoever it was kicked me again and yelled, "Of course, it's warm! Your bed's on fire! Get up!" I opened my eyes and saw three-foot flames coming out of the foot of my bed. Right then I got up in a hurry.

It was Lynn who had awakened me and undoubtedly saved my life. Running around barefooted and in our nighties, we tried to put out the fire. No one came to our aid and there was no water in camp. Lynn had to go to the creek for water while I threw sand on the flames. We rescued our dunnage and my bags. Lynn's sleeping bag, being filled with highly flammable down, had burned completely. The big canvas tarps had resisted the flames and were partly responsible for our survival. My two bags had several plate sized holes burned in them. With the fire out we soon became aware of the cold. We took the bags apart and each took one. That way each of us had at least some kind of bag for the rest of the night. We both jumped back into our remaining bedrolls and hoped desperately that our frozen bare feet might eventually thaw.

Lying there wondering that none of the almost forty people sleeping all around us had heard the fuss, I became aware that someone was hollering at us. I peeked out far enough to see that it was one of our guests who was in her own bag across the fire from us. I assumed that she was trying to get our attention, perhaps to ask if we were okay or maybe to offer assistance. That was nice but I wasn't going to get out of what little bag I had to talk to her. Lynn sat up, and the woman said, "Before you go back to bed, put some more logs on the fire. I'm getting a little cold over here." I instantly saw red, but to my amazement Lynn never said a word. She got up, walked barefoot to the wood pile and replenished the fire. She returned to her bedroll and without a word went to bed. It must have been shock or something because about thirty seconds later Lynn sat straight up in bed and yelling, "What do you mean, put another log on the fire…" and proceeded to tell the guest what she thought of her.

The next morning was cold enough that we were bundled up in our coats and scarves while we were cooking breakfast. The bottom of my old gray coat was burned off in big black scallops. That made me feel kinda queasy since I had been using it as my pillow last night. Pretty soon everyone was asking about the rather unusual trimmings on the coat. Lynn and I just allowed as how we had found a new way to sleep warm in the mountains.

SWISS STEAK

As a back country pack cook you don't just make it up as you go along. Taking into consideration your itinerary, the 'shelf life' of your fresh, the food preferences of the guests, the weight of your supplies, and the costs, you carefully plan a menu for all of your meals. Then you work out supply and equipment lists to match. Some of the bigger outfits have standardized menus which make having the right stuff available at the station a lot easier. Since preparation often involves freezing or pre-cooking certain items Rock Creek even has an outfitter who has everything ready for you. Since you often end one trip late on Saturday and start the next one on Sunday morning, the outfitter is greatly appreciated.

In the old days at Mt. Whitney, Barbara Jefferson and I would sit down and make up the menus and lists for each individual trip. In the summer of 1967 we were planning an 18 day trip. It was for a small group of hikers and the crew would just be Norrie Livermore and myself. Since coming up with 17 different dinners that will fit into your plans isn't always easy, we ended up trying to think of just one more meal that I could make. Barbara suggested Swiss steak. I was ashamed to admit it, but not only didn't I know how to make it; I didn't even know what it was. Barbara said not to worry that she would add the necessary supplies to the list and give me a recipe before we left. It turns out that the reason I had no experience with Swiss steak goes clear back to my parents' honeymoon. It seems as how my mom fixed just that dish for my dad during their first week of marriage. My dad, being new to the marriage game, told her that it wasn't nearly as good as the Swiss steak his mother made. My mother, knowing how to hold a grudge, never made it again in the twenty or so years they were married, thus depriving her five offspring of any acquaintance with said dish.

Actually Swiss steak is simple, cheap and old-fashioned. You just take some round steak and beat it until it's somewhat tenderized. Then you coat it with flour and a little salt and pepper, and brown it on both sides. Leaving the browned meat in the pan you add some canned tomatoes, sliced onions, sliced bell peppers and spices. Then you simmer it an hour or so until it's tender and serve it with mashed potatoes to soak up the juice. Too bad I didn't know that back in '67.

Well anyway, during the hectic preparations for this trip both Barbara and I forgot about the recipe. The entire itinerary for the trip had to be changed due to the heavy snow in the high country that summer. We went in over Paiute Pass, swung south to Evolution Meadow, worked back north through Selden Pass and Bear Creek, came out Mono Pass, then trucked the stock south to Lone Pine, and did a loop from Cottonwood to Whitney Portal. The trip provided many amazing memories including Norrie swimming naked down the creek at North Lake to retrieve a runaway watermelon, a big wreck of his green string of mules on their first bridge crossing at Paiute Creek, the girl in the bikini at the top of Mono Pass, getting Tommy mad because we came out at the wrong roadhead at Rock Creek, and walking out over Whitney with an injured horse. All very interesting stories, but back to the Swiss steak.

It wasn't until we were several days into the trip before I had time to sit down and go over my menus and supplies. It was then that I realized that I hadn't gotten the recipe from Barbara. First I panicked and then I went into total denial. We spent two really beautiful days at Evolution Meadows and three very rainy days at Rosemarie Meadow, and I didn't think once about Swiss steak. If there had been any women on the trip, I might have asked one of them what their recipe for Swiss steak was like. Since the guests were all men who didn't seem to have much interest in cooking, I had no chance of weaseling the necessary information out of anyone. Norrie pointed out to me that I was acting like a total bitch and said that he sure hoped I would get past whatever was bothering me. Adopting the attitude that with luck I might not live until the eighth night of the trip, I tried to pretend that nothing was wrong.

On the eighth day we moved down Bear Creek to Kip Camp. During the preceding nights I had imagined that by the time we reached this camp, the process of elimination would have at least shown me which of the remaining food items went to make up Swiss steak. No such luck. Arriving at camp, I still had no idea what to do for dinner. So instead of setting up my kitchen and getting to work, I looked for ways to stall. I noticed that the camp, being right on the John Muir Trail, was heavily used and pretty trashy. That was it! I couldn't possibly fix dinner until I had picked up every piece of trash in camp! Here were some cigarette butts, some pieces of foil, part of a candy bar wrapper... Pick them all up. There....a piece of wire, a bottle cap. Yes, yes, much too much to do to start dinner yet.

Then I picked up an empty book of matches by the fire pit. For those of you too young to remember, lots of companies used to give away books of matches with advertising in them. Hunts Foods even advertised their products by putting recipes using their stuff in match books. This book had a picture of a can of tomatoes on it. Not even noticing that, I automatically flipped it open to see if there were any matches left. The matches were all gone, but there staring me in the face was recipe for...yup; you got it...Swiss steak. Swear to God.... Not making it up.....Right in the place and at the moment when I most needed it, there it was, a recipe for Swiss steak.

Quickly getting to work, I set up my kitchen. I got out the stuff for dinner including round steak, tomatoes, bell peppers, and onions. Putting the coffee pot on, I was smiling. Peeling the potatoes, I kept giggling. Tasting the Swiss steak just before I served it, I was laughing right out loud. Norrie though I had lost my mind and allowed as how it might have been better if I just stayed bitchy. Like I said before, Swiss steak isn't a very fancy dish, but I was sure happy to be fixing it that night. It was pretty good, too.

OL' WRIST BREAKER

Looking over the Mt. Whitney Pack Trains stock at the start of the season, there was one new horse that really caught your eye. Big, put together right, a black gelding with socks all the way around, I allowed as how he would be a nice one to ride this summer. The packer leaning on the fence next to me mentioned that the gelding's name was Marty, but since he broke Ken's wrist everyone just called him Ol' Wrist Breaker. It seemed that anything unusual caused this horse to just bust in two. During the roundup, Ken had tried to rope off of him. Guess he'd never been roped off of before, so Ken was set to do the rest of the season one handed. I allowed as how I hoped I wouldn't have to ride him that summer after all.

Seemed that most of us in the crew of Mt. Whitney Pack Trains felt the same way, and Marty hardly got used at all that summer. It was mid September, on a three day Whitney trip when I saw him again. It was the end of the season and most of the stock was pretty wore out so the packer was using Marty.

We were camped at Outpost Camp when a hiker looking for help found us. He was the leader of a boys' group who had to leave one of his boys at Crabtree Meadows because the kid had emphysema and couldn't hike out. That late in the year meant no rangers and no radios in the backcountry. We knew that there wasn't anybody back at the pack station either. Since the packer had to take our guests and their stuff out, the only one left to get the sick boy was the fat little cook: me. Right away I figured out that the best horse to haul a sick little boy was Tequila. He was small but tough and dependable. The only horse in good enough shape to haul me over the mountain and back was good Ol' Wrist Breaker.

We headed up the trail leading Tequila. Marty was on his best behavior, but he was always like that until something blew him up. According to the boys, that could be anything out of the ordinary. At 12,000 feet we reached the 99 switchbacks and I started loose herding Tequila in front of me. When we got to Weeping Rock near the 55th switchback, I watched Tequila tip toe across and realized that this 30 foot section of trail which usually ran with water was, instead, frozen solid. Looking down the 400 foot drop under us, I decided that Marty and I would both have a better chance if we did this separately. Not realizing that we were already on the ice, I swung down on the inside. Next thing I knew I was lying flat on my back on the ice, my feet hanging off in space, looking straight up at the horse's belly. As I unsuccessfully tried to scramble out on the inside, I wondered if Marty might not consider this one of those out-of-the-ordinary things worth blowing up about. He didn't move a muscle. Unable to climb the ice, I had to roll over, scrabble around, and crawl on my side along the few inches of ice-covered rock between his right hind leg and the cliff edge. Ol' Wrist Breaker never even stirred. I was really beginning to like this horse.

The rest of the trip in towards Crabtree was pretty easy if you don't count balancing two horses in a pile of talus while 25 boy scouts and 25 burros work their way around you as being any big deal. I found the poor little sick boy at Guitar Lake. He was 6'4", weighed 210 pounds, and seemed more stoned than sick. Most likely, he had the pulmonary edema that came with altitude sickness. Regardless, I figured if I just got him on Tequila, that little horse would bring him out safe. The real problem was his backpack. It was huge and must have weighed 50 or 60 pounds. There was no way Tequila could carry the boy and his pack. I knew Marty could carry the weight so I put it on and crawled aboard. It stuck up a good six inches above my head which worried me but didn't seem to bother good old Marty. We started up the long pass toward home. The kid didn't seem to have any idea what was going on, but Tequila took care of him.

Between Trail Junction and Trail Crest there is a piece of trail that I have always hated. It is narrow and there is an overhanging rock. While you are ducking that rock, you can look 500 feet straight down just past your right boot. Coming up on this spot, I began to imagine that I would catch that big, old pack on the overhanging rock and fall 500 feet before I bounced the first time. Trying to concentrate on arguing myself out of panicking by being calm and logical, I was two inches from the rock when I realized that I really was going to hit the damn thing. I grabbed for the horn. Too late! The pack hit. I was shoved onto Marty's rump, my spurs buried in his flanks, my fingernails buried in the bottom of a saddlehorn I couldn't quite reach. Wedged in place, looking 500 feet straight down at the cliffs and talus below me, I let out a panicked scream. If ever a horse had cause to blow up, this was it. But Marty didn't blow up. He just froze in place.

There was nothing I could do but wait to die. After a few more minutes, Marty let out a sigh and began to ease backwards. He leaned back just until the pack slipped loose from the rock. With the grace of a dancer, he swung his body, me, and the pack out and around the overhanging rock. Then with one dazed pack cook still sitting on his rump, Marty walked quietly up the trail. Good Ol' Wrist Breaker.

When I regained my wits, I quickly scrambled back into the saddle. I checked on the kid on Tequila. He didn't seem to realize anything had happened, but Tequila was bringing him along fine. We topped the pass and headed on down the mountain. At Weeping Rock, we both got off and led our animals gingerly across the ice. Getting back on with that pack was getting to be a major pain, but by now I was determined to deliver it safely along with its owner. As we jumped down all the big steps in the trail near Consultation Lake, I could feel the pack putting black and blue marks above my kidneys with each jump. I was really starting to hate that thing. Late in the day we finally reached the pack station where I handed the kid and his pack over to his grateful group leader. Being the only crew member there, I finished the evening by finding the 25 visiting burros a corral and some feed, taking care of our stock, and giving Marty and Tequila a big bait of extra grain.

I guess that's the end of the story except for a couple of things I heard later. The first is that the damn kid's damn backpack was stolen out of the campground that very night. I should have left the damn thing up on the mountain. The second is a whole lot sadder. That fall Marty bucked off a deer hunter and hurt him bad. The hunter got well, but Marty was sold onto the killer truck. It broke my heart when I heard that. I guess no one will ever know why he chose to save my life twice on that single day. I hope where he is now is all clear streams and green meadows. So long, Ol' Wrist Breaker.

MOVING STOCK TO THE ELDER

Not all pack station stories involve mule strings in the high lonesome. A fair number of the more exciting tales took place while moving stock between the high country station and winter pastures in the Owens Valley. From the beginning of the packing days horses and mules were driven in mixed herds from the open sage brush flats to the trailhead corrals.

One of my first experiences moving stock this way was, of course, with Mt. Whitney Pack Trains. It was late fall and time to move the animals down from the mountains. That late in the season most of the crew was gone for the year. About the only people left were my boss Tommy Jefferson, his wife Barbara, their kids, an occasional neighbor, and, of course, me, Irene, the little fat cook and cowboy wannabe. In this case we were moving 26 head of horses from the pack station at Whitney Portals to a field in the Alabama Hills called the Elder. I still have many questions about this ride-such as why we didn't start earlier in the year, why we didn't start till 4 PM that day, and why the only other person riding was a 12 year old girl. Since I'll never know the answers to these questions, I'll just have to wonder.

The trail left the pack station on the Portals Road, cut through the campgrounds, got back on the road to ride the big switchbacks down the front of the scarp, followed the road for three or four miles across the flats, picked up an old trail through the Alabama Hills, crossed the Horseshoe Meadows Road, took an old dirt road to the fence on the Elder and followed the fence line to the gate on the far corner.

When you loose herd a bunch like this, one person rides point and the other pushes drag. All the point rider has to do is stay ahead of the leaders so the herd will follow them. On the flats this can be really difficult, but on the road it should have been easy. So I told little Kathy to ride point while I gathered and pushed the rest. We left the station around four in the afternoon with Kathy in the lead. Not over ten minutes later as we worked through the campground, I could see that at least eight head were in front of Kathy. I hollered at her to cut across and get ahead of them. Instead she started crying and rode back to where I was. She said that she was afraid and couldn't do it. Realizing that I had made a bad mistake by putting her on point, I told her to push the back horses while I took the point. Cutting through the campsites like a mad woman, I managed to get in front of the leaders and point everyone down the road where it narrowed along the canyon wall. Thinking that everything was now okay, I looked for Kathy to give her a big thumbs up. She wasn't there. Apparently she was upset enough that she just rode back to the station.

Realizing that it was just me and a bunch of loose horses left with close to ten miles to cover, I thought real hard about panicking. How could I lead them from the front and push them from the back all at the same time? Since we were now on a narrow mountain road with steep hillside above and below us, the horses pretty much had to stay on that road. Did I mention there were also some cars on that same road? The ones in front of us were no real problem. They just pulled to the side and waited while the horses streamed by them. The ones behind us actually served as my drag riders. While they waited for a chance to squeeze around us, they pushed the horses for me.

I was feeling pretty good about how this was working out. I never had to move faster than a high trot to stay ahead of even the snortiest ponies. Since my horse, Dooley, was a big bay standard bred trotter, we could move pretty fast at a trot. In fact we trotted much of the first five miles. This was when I learned that you never wear dangly earrings while pushing stock. Liked to beat my ears to a pulp. Distracted by all of this we were almost to the bottom of the switchbacks before I noticed we were losing the light.

By the time we were out on the flats, it was pitch black. Now I couldn't see the horses behind me, but I could hear their hoof beats on the pavement. I couldn't figure out anything else to do so I just crossed my fingers and kept going. By this time the stock had pretty much settled down and lined out behind us. I just let Dooley find the way and listened for the ones following. Every once in a while a car would come by and the headlights would let me catch a glimpse of the stock. Couldn't be sure, but it seemed like I still had most of them.

After following the road for several miles, I was supposed to find a dirt trail that cut across through the Alabama Hills. I had never been that way before and would probably have had a hard time finding the trail even in the daylight. I was worried but I also knew that if I missed the trail, I could get where we were headed by staying on the road. It would be quite a bit longer, but we wouldn't be totally lost. I needn't have worried about it; Dooley was taking care of things. He suddenly made a right into the sagebrush and walked off across the flat. Obviously, he had found our trail.

Moving away from the occasional headlights on the road, we traveled with no light except for the multitude of stars flung across the deep black sky. Without the sound of hooves on pavement to tell me where the horses were, I just had to hope they were still with me. It was quiet and the stars were beautiful. My horse was moving right along and I was even starting to enjoy our little ride in the dark. If you have never seen the stars in the Eastern Sierra, you have never seen stars. Gazing at the multitude of brilliant lights overhead, I was startled when fully a fourth of them directly above me suddenly disappeared. Scared me so bad I nearly bailed off my horse before I realized that whatever was blocking the stars wasn't moving. The trail we were on had finally led us into the towering rocks of the Alabama Hills and my horse walked in under one. It was 30 feet tall and overhanging.   My heart was pounding and I was extremely grateful that there was no one there to see me get scared to death by a rock. Of course Dooley was there, but I didn't figure he was likely to tell anyone.

Before too much longer, I came to the place where the trail crossed Horseshoe Meadows Road. The crossing was on a blind hill, so Barbara was there with her car's headlights on so we wouldn't get hit when we crossed. Looking back at the animals behind us, I was pleased to see that there were still quite a few horses there.

Dooley took me down a dirt road to a barb wire fence. He turned right along the fence and kept going. Eventually we crossed a small stream and a boggy meadow. When we came up out of that low spot, I could see truck headlights up ahead. I sure hoped that would be someone waiting for us at the gate into the Elder field. Sure enough, it was Tommy's pickup and trailer, and he was holding the gate open for us.

Feeling smug about arriving with at least some of the stock, I rode proudly into the lights. I smiled and looked back. Damn!! I was all alone. There wasn't one single horse behind me! That was impossible. I had seen them at the crossing and heard them most of the rest of the way. Spinning Dooley around, I headed back. It didn't take us long to find them. They had stopped by the creek for a little snack. Pushing them ahead of me down the road and into the light, I started counting. I had 24 head. That was two less than I started with, but all things considered that seemed pretty good.

Tommy was counting too and with a big smile said, "Well, that's all of them." It seemed that he already had the two missing animal. The old Ely mare had followed Kathy back to the station and was still there. Little Dusty, a notorious bunch quitter, had left us when we were still on the road. Tommy had come across the palomino gelding strolling down the pavement all by himself. Tommy had caught him and brought him along in the trailer.

Glad that the horses were all okay, I unsaddled my partner, Dooley, and turned him into the Elder with his buddies. Climbing into the pickup, I was pretty much glad this workday was over. I looked at Tommy and said, "Let's call it a day." He grinned and said, "Okay, it's a day." Yeah, the boss was a funny guy.

BEULAH AND JAFO:
OR HOW I LEARNED TO RIDE
MULES IN THE MOUNTAINS

Part of the way of life in the high lonesome is to live as if it was a hundred years ago. There are no roads and transportation usually has four legs. Water comes out of the stream, you cook over a campfire, and you sleep on the ground. Your alarm clock is the change of light as the dawn tints the peaks around you. Entertainment is singing and story telling around the campfire. After 40 years of working in the packing business, it is interesting to note that even in a life dedicated to living in the past, there is constant change. Styles change and equipment changes. When I first came here, you wore jeans in the summer and shot gun chaps in the cold weather. Twenty years ago packers on the west side of the Sierra started wearing chinks, knee-length summer chaps. For a few years east side packers made fun of the little "girlie chaps". Eventually they caught on and now everyone wears chinks, all the time and everywhere. Back in the beginning men packed and the only way a woman could work in the backcountry was to cook. Now everyone learns to pack. But one of the biggest changes was in the evolution of mules from purely pack animals to deluxe riding animals.

Back when I started working for Mt. Whitney Pack Trains, you rode horses and packed mules. Out of the 30 head of mules we used, exactly two were broke to ride. One was the former boss' personal riding animal. The other was one of a matched pair of molly mules. Since they were a near perfect match, it seemed like every time they tried to use Judy to ride, some fool would get out Sue by mistake and there would be a hell of a rodeo. Nowadays at Rock Creek about a third of the mules are good, gentle riding animals. It gives the outfit a lot of flexibility since you have about 20 head that can ride or pack depending on what you need that day. The individual packer out in the backcountry also benefits, as he can replace an injured riding animal with a mule from his string. I'm sure the prejudice against riding mules came from the guys who packed in the summer and cowboyed the rest of the year. Mule people don't like to admit it, but mules aren't fast enough to be really good at working cattle out on the flat.

The other reason there weren't many riding mules in the old days was that no one put in the time to train them. When you bought a new mule back then, if you were lucky it came halter broke. If he was already halter broke then it was time to break him to pack. To do that you snubbed him up to a post, blindfolded him, and tied up a foot. With him restrained this way, you put on his pack saddle, loaded him and tied down the hitch. If you were smart, this first load was something unbreakable that didn't rattle. Then you removed the restraints and tied him into your string. You would probably want him at the end of your string and would likely put double lead ropes on him. Aside from that you expected him to go down the trail just like the rest of the string. That was pretty much it for mule training in the old days.

Occasionally one of the old boys who was a little smarter than the others would go ahead and make himself a riding mule.

Mules are surer footed and way more sensible than the average horse when it comes to dealing with the high, rugged trails of the Sierra. When Bruce Morgan was the boss at Mount Whitney, he made himself just such a mule. Her name was Beulah. Mules are long lived, so years later when Bruce's kids were running the outfit, Beulah was still there. She was considered the best animal in the outfit and it was counted an honor to get to ride her. The only time I ever got to ride her was on one Whitney loop. One of our guests was a big, self-important man who had made it clear, even before he arrived, that he expected only the best. So our boss, Tommy Jefferson, gave him the best, Beulah. Of course, he wasn't smart enough to know what a good deal he had. When we arrived at our first night's camp, he called Tommy over and complained. He knew from watching cowboy movies that only idiots and rubes rode mules. He said that he was insulted and carefully explained to us all that he was very rich and therefore worthy of respect. Only he didn't say it all that polite. Tommy didn't bother to explain that he had the best animal in the outfit. He just gave him my horse and let me ride Beulah for the next eight days.

Those eight days were my first experience mule riding. What a pleasure! Smooth and careful in the rocks, calm and sensible in any situation, she made even the good horses pale by comparison. The only hitch in riding her was that the bridle I had brought for the short necked horse I started the trip on only had a roping rein. That's a single short rein made so when you drop it on a roping horse's neck there is no extra to get caught in your dallies. Beulah was a big, long necked, low headed mule. That meant that to hold that short rein I pretty much had to stick my arm way out on her neck. It was pretty uncomfortable. So one day I got to thinking how well Beulah knew these trails having been on them for decades. She was so solid that you couldn't have shoved her off the trail with a bulldozer. Then I had the brilliant thought that I could probably just drop that rein on her neck and let her do the driving.

Putting Beulah in charge worked out pretty well until the day we rode to the top of Mt. Whitney. The top of Whitney is pretty high, about 14,496 feet, and parts of the trail are real hairy. Now you wouldn't think that someone who rode that kind of country for a living would be afraid of heights, but I was (and am). Moments of gut-clenching fear are just the price you pay for getting to live the best life the world has to offer. The really bad parts of the Whitney trail are the 99 switchbacks, the overhanging rock, and the windows. With Beulah under me, I worried a lot less than usual about these places. Now the windows are sections of trail that go between the Keeler Needles and the top of the peak. Each of them is a knife edge where both sides of the trail drop straight off; a thousand feet to the east and 500 feet to the west. By this point my confidence in Beulah was so great that the rein was still down on her neck, even in a spot like that. Well, you see a piece of the trail had fallen out on the east side. That means that there was a big, ol' hole in the trail. The trail was plenty wide enough to get around it, but Beulah had other ideas. She hadn't seen that hole before and it made her curious.

Much to my surprise and horror, Beulah ambled on over to that hole and stuck her nose in it to see what it was. I would have pulled her back away from it, but when she put her head down, the reins slid right down behind her ears. Sitting on her back, frozen in terror, I stared at the following view: my saddlehorn, Beulah's neck and ears, a thousand feet of empty air, and two little lakes way down at the bottom of the cliff. Not wanting to startle or off balance her I just sat there until she got tired of looking down. Eventually she backed away from the hole and went on up the trail. A few minutes later we reached the open flat at the top of the mountain. All the guests and the rest of the crew walked around looking off at the incredible spaces surrounding us. I spent my time rummaging through my saddlebags and pockets until I found enough pieces of string and leather to tie

together to make a cheater for my reins. It seems that letting
Beulah drive wasn't quite as good an idea as I first thought.

Some other mule memories happened years later at Rock
Creek and involve a mule named Jafo. I was in at Pioneer
Basin at a base camp. Since I was staying in the same camp for
a week, they had taken my riding animal out with the empty
mules. Being stuck in camp for a week isn't so bad when camp
is a beautiful spot overlooking Mono Creek canyon and backed
by a great little swimming lake. The day before we were due to
come out I got one of those dreaded notes from the boss, Herb
London. It said, "I hope you have a change of clothes because
you're not coming out tomorrow. You will stay where you are
and join an outbound, seven day, traveling trip. We will send
you something to ride." They did send me a horse, but he got
hurt coming in over the pass. There were no extra horses, and I
wasn't real thrilled to think about walking the next few moves.

My packer on this trip was Jim Brumfield, a hell of a hand.
He told me that he wasn't real sure that there were any broke
mules in his string, but that he would go look. He came back
and said that he seemed to remember that Sid was supposed to
be broke when the outfit bought him. Jim said he would go top
him off for me. Pretty soon, from the direction of the picket line,
there came a lot of yelling and crashing and a big cloud of dust.
After a while Jim came back to camp, covered in dust and with a
small branch sticking out of the collar of his shirt. He said, "Sid
don't ride." He thought a little while and then allowed as how
Jafo might possibly be broke and that he would go and top her
off for me.

After a while Jim returned with the news that Jafo wasn't
broke either, but that I could probably ride her. When Jim rode
her it was obvious that while she had never been ridden before,
she considered a person to be just one more pack load. As long
as you lined her up behind another animal she would just carry
you along as she followed down the trail. So that's what we did

all week. Wherever we needed to go, we just put one other rider ahead of us and off we went. The only snag occurred on a day ride to Third Recess. To get from Mono Creek up to the recess, you had to scramble your animal up a steep hill covered in fist-sized, round rocks. I was riding at the back of the group. About half way up that hill the gal in front of me dropped her hat. I jumped off and picked it up for her, but she just kept going. Abandoned by her equine buddies, Jafo started to panic. I tried to swing up on her as she took off, but the rock under my right foot rolled and I fell. My left foot hung up in the stirrup and I was being dragged up the hill. It seemed like one of those moments when your life should flash before your eyes, but I guess mine wasn't interesting enough. Luckily, after only a half dozen jumps, my foot pulled loose and I was left sitting in the rocks, basically undamaged. I limped on up the hill where I caught up with the group. I returned the hat to its owner and reclaimed my mule. Jafo didn't seem to care that I was back on her. I guess it didn't matter to her what kind of odd load you put on her as long as you didn't leave her behind.

The only other time I rode Jafo came several years later. It was a quiet layover day at the end of a long, hard trip. This was the same trip where we tangled with the bears at Cora Creek and where I forgot to bring the silverware, but those are two other stories. Our riders on this trip didn't want to go on day rides on the layover days. It was a rest day and they wanted to rest. That meant the packers, Dave Dohnel and Richie Engle, didn't have to guide or saddle. They could just hang around camp or fish or sleep. I guess they got bored, because it wasn't much after lunch time when it became obvious that they were up to something. What they had in mind was "The First Annual Graveyard Meadows Mule Race". That the meadow was long and flat, a rarity in the central Sierra, was likely what gave them the idea. None of the people on this trip were riding mules so any race competitors would have to come out of the pack strings.

The boys had their eyes on Opal and CJ, two big black, half thoroughbred mules. Both mules were well broke and fast. It was a challenge of the experienced-packer-in-his-prime (Dave) against the eager-new-packer (Ritchie). I whined to Dave that I wanted to race, too. Rather than reminding me that lowly old lady cooks had no place in this macho race, he just said there weren't any other broke mules available. I asked him if I could race if I found something to ride. He said that I could. I went to the picket line to look over the mules, and there asleep on the line was a little, round bay molly. It was Jafo.

I told Dave that I was going to use Jafo, and he got pretty excited. Mainly he told me that I couldn't use her because she had never been ridden before and she would kill me. I told him that I had ridden her before. He said that I had her mixed up with some other mule, because no one had ever ridden her before. Tired of the argument and being pretty snotty by nature, I just said I didn't care if she'd never been ridden before; I was going to ride her today. Dave tried to talk me out of it, but I just saddled her up. Just before I got on her, Dave allowed as how I had more balls than he did. Since Dave was the kind of guy who could ride anything with hair, I got kind of a kick out that. Of course, I knew that Jafo would just pack me around like she had before.

Now the next problem we faced was that you can't win a race by following behind another animal, which was the only way Jafo would go anywhere. So we tried a little training session out on the meadow. I squeezed her, she just stood there. I kicked her, nothing. I popped her with a stick, no change. Finally, I clucked to her and she took off. I guess she surprised me because Dave was laughing pretty hard at the look on my face. Now that we actually had some motion, the problem changed to how does a short, fat, old woman on a little fat mule beat two athletic young men on well trained, speed bred mules. We couldn't out run them so maybe we could out think them. The answer to our problem seemed to hinge on the fact that all the horses were tied to the picket line, which was off in the trees to the left of the midpoint of our race course. Knowing a little about mules, I figured that, given a chance, our racers would head for the picket line.

Jafo and I took our starting place to the far right of the other two animals. We were off! As the other two sped off up the meadow, I clucked Jafo into a nice lope and cranked her nose around to my right knee. Wanting to go left to the horses, but with her neck turned to the right, Jafo made a fairly straight line up the meadow. Ahead of us Opal and CJ, running full out, made an abrupt left into the trees. As Jafo and I loped on by we could see a lot of commotion over by the picket line. Before too long the mules and their riders came tearing out of the trees and back up the meadow. They passed us like we were standing still. Then realizing that the race was just between the two of them, the guys loosened their reins for more speed. Recognizing an opportunity when it was presented, both mules made another sharp left turn back toward the picket line. By the time they got out of the trees for the second time, Jafo and I were loping slowly across the finish line. As I headed Jafo, winner of the "First Annual Graveyard Meadow Mule Race," back to camp, my grin turned into a laugh. It was one of those moments when you started laughing and just couldn't stop. I laughed all the way back to camp. I laughed so hard that I almost fell off when we crossed the creek. Dave just looked at me and said, "Dammit, Irene, I hate it when you have this much fun!"

If I was telling this around the campfire, by now it would be burning down to coals and we would all head off for our bedrolls. So I'll have to wait for another time to tell you about Dodger, Julie, Abby, Jasper, Art, Turnip and all the other mules that helped shape my life in the high lonesome.

ONE TOUGH TRIP

Sitting around the campfire after a long day in the Sierra, the crew and the guests provide their own amusement. Occasionally you work for a boss who allows as how it's part of your job to be down right entertaining. With several after dinner drinks under your belt, you start to thinking you're a lot more entertaining than you actually are. If you're lucky, someone is good enough on the guitar to make it worth while packing the darn thing all those miles. Sometimes you get a good singer, a real live cowboy poet, or a great storyteller. When you're not so lucky, you get a group that can't sing and brought the songbooks to prove it. Once I had some people who thought it was entertaining to read aloud from "Place Names of the High Sierra", pretty dry listening. When you're the old pack cook and your "repertory" consists of two jokes and one off-color song, you pretty much limit yourself to telling packing stories. While stories are fun around the campfire, a really good trip is one that doesn't provide any new stories about adventures in the high lonesome. A really good trip is peaceful and quiet with everything going just right. The more trouble you get into on a trip, the more stories you have to tell. One of the worst trips I ever took was going from Agnew Meadows to Yosemite Valley when I was working for

Reds Meadows. This trip was only five days long, but it provided six or seven new campfire tales. These stories are from that trip.

STORY ONE

On this trip we left out from Agnew Meadows. The trip was set to go all the way to the floor of Yosemite Valley in just five days. That meant we would have five long moves and no layover days. Our guests were five former marines who figured they were tougher than 6-year-old jerky. Our packer was a young man named Matt who had just gotten his degree in psychology. He had worked his way through school by packing in the summers and was thinking that this might be his last trip. I was the pack cook, which seemed to be one more woman than these "real men" wanted on their trip.

We traveled up the high trail from Agnew to Thousand Island Lake. By the time we reached the lake it became obvious that we were in for a serious storm. Matt was doing some bragging on his wet weather equipment. He had a full-length waterproof duster, good gloves, and gaiters to keep the water from running into his boots. He had one of those plastic hat protectors that most of the boys called "hat condoms". Being at a financially precarious time in my life, my equipment consisted of a plastic poncho, the kind you get at the sporting goods store for $2.99. Better than nothing, but just barely.

Island Pass is on the John Muir Trail between Thousand Island Lake and Rush Creek. It's a low, easy pass and one of the most beautiful spots around. The top of the pass gives you an incredible view of the lake and Banner and Ritter Peaks at its head. The pass itself is an alpine garden of wildflowers scattered through the rocks around several tarns.

The storm broke just before we reached the top of Island Pass. Wind came screaming off the peaks. Waves with whitecaps thrashed across the lake below us. Hail pounded down directly in our faces. Our horses tried desperately to turn their faces away from the storm. We had to fight them to keep them moving and on the trail. Then the lightening started striking all around us. I've always had the habit of counting seconds between the lightening and the thunder. Five seconds means that the lightening is hitting a mile away. In this case the lightening was so close that you couldn't count to one, and all you really wanted to do was get down off the ridge. We did get off the pass without being hit. As we started down the mountainside towards Rush Creek, the lightening slacked off, but, boy howdy, did it rain. It rained so hard that the entire hillside was a moving sheet of water. It was impossible to tell where the trail was. So we just sloshed down the hill hoping we were somewhere close to where we were supposed to be.

We were fortunate and reached the bottom of the canyon within a few feet of where we needed to be. We found the place where the trail cut through a big slot in the rocks and crossed our first stream crossing. The creek coming down from Davis Lakes is a dinky little creek normally eight feet across and less than a foot deep. By this time it was twice its normal size with a powerful current. I noticed that each horse had to scramble for his footing when he hit that current. This made me nervous because waiting for us a mile or so upstream was the Rush Creek crossing. Rush Creek is a big, serious creek. Normally the crossing is 20 feet across and up to your horse's belly in the deeper spots. Just below the crossing, there is a steep stretch of creek where the water crashes through boulders making white water for more than two miles until it reaches Waugh Lake. Of course that's what it's like when the sky isn't dumping torrents of rain down on you.

When we got to the crossing, Matt stopped and spoke to our guests. He explained what lay below us and warned them how dangerous the crossing would be. Like good ex-marines everywhere, they replied that they weren't afraid of crossing a little water. Matt gave them a warning that I have never heard before or since. He said that if your horse was swept downstream by the current, your only chance would be to pull yourself around on the upstream side and hang on. If you could do that and manage to hold on while the rocks beat your horse to death, his body might protect you long enough for you to reach the lake's calmer waters. At this point the marines seemed to get a whole lot quieter. After all this preparation, the actual crossing went fairly smoothly if you don't count riding through freezing waves that came up past your knees and got your boots full of water. The water was deep and wide but we made it without any real problems.

With only a few more miles to go and only one little steam crossing left, I started to look forward to getting into camp. The rain had stopped, but the streams were still running high. Though Matt looked smugly warm and dry, I was cold, wet and freezing. I checked on the guys and realized that at least two of them were pretty close to having hypothermia. I figured they would be okay as soon as they had a campfire and some warm dinner.

At last we came to the meadow where we would camp. All we had to do was ride across a little bit of meadow, go over an itty-bitty creek, ride up the bank and around behind the trees and we would be there. Though the stream was twice as large as normal, it was still way too small to worry about. At least that's what we thought. Matt rode across the water and up the bank and waited for his five mules to cross behind him. In one of those incidents that make packing such an interesting line of work, the string clothes-lined his number three mule. As she crossed the water, the two mules in front of her jumped up the bank at the exact moment the two behind her became frightened and pulled back. This jerked her off her feet and she spun upside down on the taut ropes. Pinned on her back by the weight of her load, her head was under the water. Matt leaped off his horse and without a single thought to the fact that he was the only dry person there, dove into the creek to save his mule. Struggling to hold her head above water, he finally pried his knife out of his pocket and cut her lead rope. By that time she had lost enough of her load in the stream that when she was also cut free from the mules behind her, she managed to get to her feet. The campsite was only 100 feet away so we soon were all safely in camp. With a roaring campfire and a warm dinner, everyone was soon set for the night. The horses and mules were grazing peacefully in the meadow. We had made it through a terrible day with no negative results, unless of course you consider the fact that there would be no salads this trip. All the lettuce and cabbage were in the third mule's load and had disappeared down stream. As it turned out, the rest of the trip was so cold and stormy that no one even missed the salads.

STORY TWO

I hate to disappoint anyone reading this, but the next day wasn't bad at all. No storms, only a few bad jokes on the trail, and no bears in camp. Over Donahue Pass to the Lyle Fork of the Tuolumne is a long rugged move, but in this case it was the nearest thing to an easy day that we had all trip. In camp that night the talk was about our next move. We would ride out down-canyon for a few miles then turn and climb up the canyon wall to the west as if we were heading for Vogelsang. Once we were up on the plateau we would climb to our campsite near Elizabeth Lake. Since we would be above 10,000 feet, campfires would be forbidden. We would use a Coleman stove to cook dinner, but hot coffee would be about all we had to keep us warm.

Everyone woke up the next morning to the sound of raindrops on the tents. Looking out you could see that the clouds were socked in so low that you could only see the bottom half of each of the pine trees in camp. The rain was a steady downpour. Violent thunderstorms like the one we encountered on Island

Pass are common in the Sierra in summer. They build up in the morning, storm during the afternoon, and are gone by evening. Rain in the morning promises a whole different kind of storm, a storm that is the tail off a hurricane down in Baja. Since the rain is continuous, people never get a chance to dry out or warm up. Some of these storms are deadly. I remember one that rained for three straight days and nights. It cost the lives of seven people in the Sierra, most from hypothermia or drowning.

Matt cleared out an area next to the kitchen and stretched an extra tarp over it. His idea was that the guests could drag their tents into this area and pack up their beds and duffle in a dry place. Then he could bring the mules in one at a time to be packed under the tarp. That way everything would be safe and dry under the mule's pack tarp before the mule went out in the rain. He went off to explain the idea to the marines who were still in their tents. It would be a lot of extra work for Matt, but considering where we were planning on camping that night, dry clothing and beds would be vital. I'm not sure where things went wrong. I guess packing up in a dry place wasn't manly enough for the macho marines. Maybe they didn't like being told what to do. Or maybe they just misunderstood Matt's instructions. Anyway, by the time they had their stuff ready to pack, everything they owned was soaking wet: clothes, tents, and sleeping bags. Matt still packed under the big tarp, but it was too late. Everything was so wet that the mule loads ran streams of water while he was packing them.

I could picture them trying to survive the coming night. It was cold enough down where we were at the time to be pretty darn sure that it was snowing up at the lake. With no campfires allowed, there would be no way to dry their beds and clothing, and no way to get warm. Even if we decided to survive by breaking the rules and having a fire anyway, the lake was too far above timberline for there to be any wood. While I fed them breakfast, I started dropping terms like snow, hypothermia, elevation, and exposure into the conversation in hopes that I might convince them to come up with a plan than didn't entail freezing to death. .Apparently ex-marines were not affected by any of these dangers.

When Matt brought in his next mule to pack, I got him aside and told him that there was a good possibility that we might lose some of these guys if we didn't get them to change their plans. The only idea I could come up with was to rent a vehicle at the roadhead and take our guests to Lee Vining where a night in a motel and the use of a Laundromat would dry everyone and everything. He said, "Don't talk to them any more. I'll take care of it". So I cleaned up the kitchen while he went back to packing. It was after 11:00 when we rolled out of camp and the rain hadn't let up one bit.

It was a little over two miles to the turn off. We just rode along cold and miserable. Looking at the horses' lowered heads and pinned ears and tails, you knew that they were miserable, too. To make things worse my cheap little poncho snagged on a dead branch and ripped right in two. I could hardly face the thought of climbing higher into colder rain and eventually slush and snow. If we just didn't turn off toward the higher country, the trial we were on would take us right to the trailhead at Tuolumne Meadows in just about two more hours. I looked at our guests who appeared as if the term hypothermia was becoming more meaningful to them by the minute. They looked more miserable than I felt.

Eventually we reach the turnoff; left would take you higher and colder, right would take you out to civilization, shelter and warmth. Matt stopped his horse and peered back at our guests whose outlook on life had been pretty much tenderized by the last hour of riding in the rain and cold. Matt just looked at them and said, "We're going out." He rode on down the right fork and everyone followed. No one said a word. By the way, did I mention that Matt was studying to be a psychologist?

STORY THREE

That night we spent in Lee Vining should have been embarrassing. After all, who ever heard of taking a pack trip to a motel? Even though Matt and I were up most of the night drying our guests' sleeping bags and clothes at the Laundromat, we were grateful to be out of the weather. Our guests might not be happy, but they were warm, dry and alive.

The next day dawned with clear blue skies. We loaded up and hauled everyone back up Tioga Pass. It was noon by the time everything was rearranged and packed on the mules. A noon start wouldn't have been so bad but we had 20 miles to ride. It was a long, beautiful ride but our butts were dragging by the time we reached Little Yosemite Valley. It was a lovely spot, but there were enough people there to start your own city. Being only seven miles from the main Yosemite Valley roadheads, it is a first night camp for the majority of hikers using that area. We got there late and had to squeeze our stock party into a small campsite on the hillside. Even crowded in like we were, another hiking party arrived later and squeezed in about 30 feet from our kitchen.

The only thing Little Yosemite had that exceeded the number of campers was the number of bears. Since most of the campers were just starting out, they had lots and lots of food. The bears thought they had died and gone to heaven. There were a number of bear boxes available, but with so many people there, the space in the boxes was severely limited. By the time we got there, there was only room for a dozen eggs and a package of bacon. The rest of our food had to be guarded in camp.

When our close neighbors arrived, they had the same problem of where to put the food. I was in our kitchen preparing dinner and they were so close that I had no choice but to overhear their discussion. There were maybe six or seven people in the group. They were very concerned about the bears and it was pretty obvious that most of them were real new to the wilderness. Where there are people who want to be led, there is always someone who wants to lead them. If they're lucky, he knows what he's doing. Not so in this case. This guy insisted that their food be hung in a tree and that he would show them exactly how it was done. When they finished, all their food was in six stuff bags hanging 30 feet up in a pine tree. They were counter balanced on a stout limb. All that was good. The fact that they were touching the trunk was not so good. All a bear would need to do to help himself to their supplies would be to climb up the trunk. I almost interrupted and told them that they were making a serious error, but stopped when I realized how much their fearless leader would resent my interference. I told myself to mind my own business and get back to cooking dinner.

During dinner I faced the fact that I was likely to have some bear troubles of my own that night. Most of our food was still in the wooden pack boxes. We still had stuff for tomorrow's breakfast and lunch for seven. We also had food for Matt and me on our return trip to Tuolumne, and we had some leftovers. I asked Matt if he was up to helping bear guard that night. He replied that he would hang the box in a tree if I could get all the remaining food in a single box. Then he said I was on my own. None of my tougher-than-nails marines volunteered to help. They all slept far away from camp so that bear noises wouldn't disturb their beauty sleep.

Matt said he was quitting the outfit after this trip and didn't care if he got fired for letting the bear get the food. Then he must have felt sorry for me because he hung the box in a tree and booby-trapped the trunk with pots and pans. Then he made a bear surprise out of dried potatoes, honey, and a whole bottle of hot sauce. He dragged the sack of garbage out of camp so when the bear got it he wouldn't mess up the rest of camp. He said that that was all he could do for me and left to sleep on the picket line.

I spread my bedroll about ten feet from the kitchen. Knowing I would be up during the night, I wore my clothes to bed. I was on my last flashlight battery so I wasn't too surprised when after about twenty minutes it went out. Now I was alone in the dark waiting for the bear. I could hear him out there by the garbage. He crunched a few cans and moved to the table. I held my breath hoping he would eat the bear surprise that was on the table. He ignored it and moved to the tree where the box was hanging. When he started to climb, he knocked down some pans. The noise told me where he was. I jumped up and pegged several large rocks in his direction while yelling at the top of my lungs. He jumped down and took off into the trees. About ten minutes later, he returned and we did an instant replay of his first visit. After three more identical visits, he discovered the tree full of food in the neighboring camp. Even without a light I could tell exactly what he was doing. First I heard his belly scraping on the tree's bark as he climbed the trunk. Then I heard ripping sounds as he clawed out the bottoms of the stuff sacks. This was immediately followed by several thuds as the food hit the ground... scraping sounds as he climbed down....munching sounds as he tucked into eating a week's supply of food for six unfortunate hikers. I dozed off and got about an hour of sleep while he was finishing off their freeze dried goodies.

Unfortunately, after he ate all their food, he seemed to remember that he had unfinished business in our camp. He returned to his ritual: crunch the cans in the garbage, sniff the table, try to climb the tree, run away when pelted with rocks, come back and do it again... and again...and again. I started to feel like crying.

Wasn't he full yet? Why wouldn't he go someplace else? Why wouldn't he eat the bear surprise? PLEASE, let him eat the bear surprise. Then like the answer to a prayer he stopped at the table and started seriously nosing around. I could hear him snuffling around the place where the surprise was waiting for him. Then I heard the most beautiful sound. He was eating it. All that dried potato and a whole jar of honey must have inspired him. He was really gulping it down until he came to the Tabasco. Then he gave a startled woof followed by a loud sneeze. Woofing and sneezing, he left our camp. Woofing and sneezing, he headed over the nearest hill. Still woofing and sneezing he disappeared into the night. Ah, silence and hopefully a little sleep.

STORY FOUR

The move from Little Yosemite to Yosemite Valley was the last day of the trip for our dudes. We would ride only about seven miles down into the main valley. Since a truck big enough to carry out 12 head of stock would not be allowed into Yosemite Valley, we would have to deadhead the stock. According to Bob Tanner, our boss at Reds Meadows, Matt and I would have to lead all the horses and mules the 27 miles back to Tuolumne Meadows. The plan was that we would leave our dudes and their duffle at the parking lot, wishing them a fond farewell and telling them how much we had enjoyed their company. There we would be met by a pick-up truck driven by some guys from Reds. They would pick up all our dude saddles, packing equipment, boxes and supplies. That would save us hours of packing time on the trail back. They would bring us bags of hay cubes so we could feed the animals on the picket line that night. All we would carry would be our personal food, dunnage, and bedrolls. Then we would return to Tuolumne taking the rest of this day and most of tomorrow.

That was the plan. This is how it actually went. The morning in camp went just fine, even the part where I got to clean up the mess the bear made. Done with breakfast, clean up, and packing, we rode out down along a big old river. I'd never been this way before and I started to wonder just how we were going to get down into the canyon. You see, much as I hate to admit it, trails on cliffs make me want to pee my pants and this old canyon was starting to look like it was leading up to something I wouldn't like much. So I asked Matt what the trail up ahead was like. Matt knew about my preference for flatter places so he understood what I was asking. "Don't worry about it," he said. "It's just a stroll down through the trees on a hillside that isn't steep at all." I smiled my gratitude at him, and we rode on.

Pretty soon I commenced to hear a roar that got louder and louder. Being in the back of the group I couldn't see much up ahead of us. I could see that there was a bridge over the river and that Matt and his mules were crossing it. Soon my horse and I were on the bridge. And the bridge was right on the lip of Nevada Falls. That's the big falls that you see in all the pictures of Yosemite. The roar was that big ol' river plunging from right under our feet hundreds of feet straight down that cliff to the floor of Yosemite Valley. If I hadn't been frozen by fear, I probably would have done something desperate.

After the bridge, we rode over some flat rock and through a grove of pines. Just as I began to relax a little we came to a spot where the trail went through a huge cliff. Yeah, you got it right, not by, over, near or along a cliff, but through it. That sucker was so steep that they had blasted a trail right through the side of it. The animals just fit into that groove and the only thing between you and a long way down was a tiny berm of rocks about 6 inches tall. When we reached the far side of that sheer cliff, the trail did indeed begin to wind down through the trees toward the floor of the valley. Though it was steep and paved with asphalt which made your animals slide, it was still a whole lot better than the earlier part of the trail. About this time I got to thinking that Matt and I were going to be riding right back up this same trail later this afternoon. It was not stacking up as the best day I'd ever had.

Later, coming out of some enormous oaks and crossing the Merced River, we rode into the parking lot at the end of the trail. Our guests took their dunnage and left to check in at the Awanee

Hotel. We looked around for the pickup truck. Boy, were we looking forward to getting rid of most of this stuff. After waiting a while we still didn't see the truck. But we did find a stack of 4 bags of hay cubes. I guessed the truck wasn't coming as there was a note pinned to one of the sacks. All it said was, "You're on your own."

We both groaned and even cussed a little. The only break we got was that, except for the dude's dunnage, we hadn't unpacked or unsaddled yet. Repacking the dunnage loads, Matt started back up the trail. I strung the empty saddle horses together, tied up their stirrups, and followed him. We needed to make the camp on Sunrise Ridge by dark.

When we got to the section of the trail that went through the cliff, I got off and led my animals on foot. I took them across strung together, as you usually only loose herd where there are a lot of switchbacks. It could have been a real mistake. Half way across, the slab-sided dun in the middle of the string pulled back and stopped the whole bunch. He tried to back up and he got his outside hind hoof off the trail. Realizing that he was in trouble, he froze and tried to feel around enough to get that foot back on the trail. His hoof was outside the berm and every time he tried to lift it back on the trail it caught on the outside of those rocks and slid back off into space. I meant to get far enough back down the string to cut some ropes which would at least save the two horses in front of him. The trail was so narrow that I couldn't squeeze past the horses between us. All I could do was hold my breath and wait. On about the eighth try he finally got his foot over the berm and back on to the trail. What a relief. After that even the bridge on the waterfall was a cinch.

STORY FIVE

Sunrise Camp is sort of a wide spot in the trail on a hillside, but at least it had water and room for a picket line. Matt unpacked and unsaddled his mules while I unsaddled the riding animals.

Matt took the animals to water while I cooked a quick dinner on the Coleman. Then he fed the stock the cubes on the picketline and we were pretty much set for the night. There was a bear cable and we hung the food we would need for the next day. Settling in for the night, I asked Matt why he had lied to me about the cliffs. He said that he knew how bad they were, but he was afraid if he told me about it, I would just quit on him. I allowed as how a person who is afraid of heights would probably do better if that person didn't have a bridge over a waterfall and a trail through a cliff come as a complete and total surprise. I also told him that this chicken-hearted girl had choked down her fear enough to ride to the top of Mt. Whitney, so maybe he had underestimated me just a tad. So much for how clever a shrink he was going to be.

Just like the night before, we had leftover food in the pack boxes. Also, like the night before, we had bears in camp. So I set my bedroll near the pack boxes and got myself some throwing rocks. I had borrowed a flashlight battery, so I was all set for the night.

As soon as I turned out the Coleman lantern, the bears came to camp. We had a big old sow with a half grown cub. Just like the night before, I ran her off and she came back. I was real careful not to get between her and the cub. After about an hour of this, several new thoughts occurred to me. First off, all I was defending was leftovers. Second, no one at the outfit cared enough about this stuff to bother to send a truck to pick it up. Third, I hadn't had any sleep the night before and today had been a pretty tough day. Fourth, it wasn't like I would be giving these bears any new bad habits, being as they obviously already knew all about stealing food. With these thoughts in mind, I dragged my bedroll about a hundred feet out of camp and went to bed. I had a good sleep and the bears had a good snack.

The next morning I had to clean up the kitchen. It was pretty interesting. The sow had put one tooth hole through each can or box. Then she apparently went ahead and ate the ones she liked and left the rest. For example, the cans of tomatoes each had one hole in them but were undamaged otherwise. The cans of peaches must have met with her approval as they had been ripped open and licked clean. All of the bear-damaged goods went into the garbage bags. The clean-up was a lot easier than staying up all night. This was the only time I ever abandoned a camp to a bear, but I must admit there have been other times when I was tempted.

STORY SIX

So now we were on the last day of our trip. Since our guests were all back in Yosemite, I couldn't blame any mistakes on them. Anything that went wrong today would have to be the fault of packer people from Reds. We had to move 12 head of stock and all our equipment from Sunrise to Tuolumne, about 17 miles. According to our boss Bob's "plan" we had to meet the truck at the rangers' station at 2 o'clock. With all the extra packing and saddling to do, it was going to be a race to get there on time.

The trail from Sunrise to Tuolumne leads through some spectacular country. Tuolumne itself is a huge high country meadow framed by low granite domes carved out by ancient glaciers. The most beautiful of these domes is Cathedral Dome. It is a long narrow dome with two matched spires at the south end. It looks very much like the European cathedrals that it is named for. From one point near the spires you can see the dome, the great meadow, and miles of pine-covered ridges stretching to the northern boundary of the park.

The trip was pretty easy, and the only time we stopped was when Matt had to repack a mule whose load was rubbing on his side. Feeling real proud of ourselves, we pulled into the ranger station corrals right at 2 o'clock. Boy, we thought we were good.

The truck that was supposed to pick us up wasn't even there yet. We tied up and started to unsaddle and unpack. Before too long everything was unloaded, and the animals were standing hipshot at the hitching rack taking a little rest. The truck still wasn't there. Matt and I found separate spots in the shade on the tack shed porch and just kinda sat and rested for a while.

It was three o'clock and still no truck. We thought about phoning Reds Meadows, but since it takes two hours to drive from there to Touloumne, we were sure that they were already on their way. We took the animals into the corral a few at a time to drink at the water trough. With nothing else to do we sat around and did nothing. In the packing business, late transportation is more of rule than a surprise, but we were starting to worry. We talked about our equipment pick up the day before. The "you're on your own" note kinda got to us. We talked about the boss booking a trip that was almost impossible to do, but by gawd, we had done it. Then they abandoned us with all that equipment, making it almost impossible to get to back to Tuolumne on time. With a good packer and tough stock, we had made it anyway. Now there was no one here to meet us.

With nothing much to do except gripe, we decided to clean up our equipment. While hauling the garbage bags to the dumpster, we also cleaned out the rest of the boxes. We found several partial bottles of whiskey left behind by our guests. Well, well…. I wonder what two tired, disgruntled packer persons should do with those. Now, instead of sitting in the shade and griping, we could sit in the shade and drink, and gripe. By the time the whiskey was gone, it was after four o'clock and we were swinging back and forth between being angry at the outfit and silly about everything else. At that point I leaped to my feet and announced that I was going to walk to the pay phone and call Reds. There must be something seriously wrong.

Since most packers don't carry change in the mountains I called collect. A little boy voice answered and accepted the collect charges. I suddenly had a sinking feeling about how several drinks under my belt might have affected my ability to dial a phone. I asked the kid where he lived, and when he said, "Arkansas", I told him to hang up quick because his mom was likely gonna kill him.

Taking considerably more care dialing, I called Reds again. This time I got it right and Bob answered. He seemed pretty cheerful so I guessed that there wasn't any emergency that would explain the lack of transportation for us. I asked him what the hell was going on. He said they were just sitting there waiting for us to call. Present circumstances and past experience told me that that was a long ways from the truth. I just told him to get the truck on the road as we were pretty tired of waiting for him. Then I went back to tell Matt the good news that we had another two hours to wait. Unfortunately, there wasn't any more whiskey left.

Now four hours of waiting is sure no big deal in many cases, but we were feeling a little mistreated. As we waited and talked, Matt said he wasn't worried about it because he was quitting this outfit anyway. As time wore on, he got quieter and I got grouchier. It was getting on into evening when the stock truck finally arrived. Bob, himself, was driving the rig. Matt just quietly started loading the stock and equipment. He never said a word. As we worked I unloaded my opinion of this entire trip on our boss. I mentioned the impossible schedule, the difficult people, the disasters along the way, his failure to pick up our stuff in Yosemite, and his tardiness in meeting us today. Matt never said a word, again convincing me that he was a whole lot brighter than I was.

I don't know if Matt ever worked for Reds after this. I do know that I didn't. I like to think that was my choice, but the fact is that Bob probably wouldn't have hired me back even if I had wanted to work there. You see, just before we got up in the truck to start the long trip back to Reds, Bob started to tell me that I shouldn't be so tough on him because he had had a bad week, too. He had hurt his heel and had to go to the hospital. Thinking about all the "fun" we had had, I felt a definite lack of sympathy. I just looked him in the eye and said that he was lucky he was crippled up because if he hadn't been, I would have used the toe of my packer boot to kick his balls up between his ears. I guess you shouldn't talk to your boss that way, but it seemed the right thing at the time.

BACKCOUNTRY COOKIN'

I tell a lot of stories about being a backcountry cook, but not many of them describe the actual cooking. Many of the required skills are lost in antiquity. If you aren't lucky enough to find an old timer who will share their knowledge with you, you're probably in trouble. There are no schools or books that teach you how to do this stuff. If you run across a book on Dutch oven cooking, it will usually start out talking about counting the number of charcoal briquettes. Right there you know the author has never cooked any farther from his house than the back yard. Well, I've been just plain lucky and over the years a lot of talented people have shared their high country cooking secrets with me. I suspect they figured that if they didn't help I might end up poisoning or starving a whole lot of folks. Anyway, I'm going to tell you a little about these people, and if you listen careful you might learn a few of their secrets.

The first cooks I worked with were at Mt. Whitney Pack Trains, where I got to work with Bruce and Charles Morgan and Barbara Morgan Jefferson. Being a butcher in the off season, Charles Morgan taught me a lot about handling meat in the high country (no pun intended). In those days, no one froze the meat or used ice chests. Meals were planned in an order based on which meat kept longest. You planned any meal requiring ground meat for the first day. Any poultry or fish had to be used in one or two days. Fresh pork was only good for about three days. From then on until around seven or eight days you used beef or lamb. After that the menu needed to include cured meats like ham and corned beef. Finally, if you went over 12 days without a resupply, you went to canned meats or dried pastas like tortellini. To make sure that your meat was fresh when you needed it, Charles taught me how to keep the meat from spoiling. Every night you would wait until after dark, unwrap all the meat, and spread it out on the table. This chilled the meat and allowed the surface to dry out. First thing in the morning, you would wrap it in fresh white butcher paper, put it in a white cloth sack, and roll it in your sleeping bag. When you were ready to use it, you unwrapped the meat and used a knife to peel off the outer layer which was like jerky. Inside, the meat was fresh and delicious. Then you would cut it into steaks, roasts, chops, or stew meat depending on what the menu called for. On one large trip Charles actually carried along the entire forequarter of a steer which he cared for in the same way. Of course, it was so large that he had to hang it up in a tree rather than put it on a table. Charles taught me several other things too, like that if you overslept when you were supposed to be up cooking, you might find a basin of ice cold water poured over your head. He also taught me some new words the day he caught me using his boning knife to chop carrots. Guess real cooks are a little sensitive about their knives.

The most memorable of my mentors was Barbara Jefferson. Barbara was born to the packing business and grew up in the little town of Lone Pine knowing everything there was to know about packing. Quiet and serene, Barbara was often the only real grown up in a business where most of the crew were still children at heart. She taught me how to be a station cook and a trail cook, how to organize menus and supply lists, how to create dishes where you had no supplies, and how to serve a dinner for thirty when you had planned for ten. She was a born teacher and would send me off to do tasks that I believed to be impossible. Once she told me to make a pineapple upside down cake for dinner. We were at Little Whitney Meadow and I knew that we hadn't planned to bring any of the things needed for such a task. Being as Barbara was the kindest person that ever lived; I knew she wouldn't set me a task that really couldn't be done. I started searching for the ingredients, keeping in mind that everything I used for this would have to be replaced for its original use. For example, I started with the canned pineapple and brown sugar that were to be the glaze for the next night's ham. I replaced that glaze with one based on apricot jam and Worcestershire sauce. We were heavy on pancake mix so I used it for the base for my cake batter. Extra flour (for thickening gravy), eggs (from breakfast) and sugar (from that meant for the coffee) kept it from rising too high and made it more cake like. Well, you get the idea. It turned out to be a cake and I was so proud I could hardly stand myself. Barbara just smiled quietly like she knew all along that I could do it.

In later years, it seemed like I learned backcountry cooking skills from everyone I worked with. I learned all the serious Dutch oven cooking skills I know in a single week from a little old man named Dink who was packing for Reds Meadows at the time. He taught me how to choose the right wood and build the right fire, how to preheat the lid while burning the wood down to coals, how to make hooks to handle the super hot lids, how to use little stones to raise the baking pan to keep it from burning, and how to estimate your cooking times. With these few skills you can bake or roast anything in a Dutch oven that you could do in your kitchen at home. Of course, it can be a little unpredictable. I remember one day when I was working for North Lake Pack and we were in at McClure Meadow. I had to make two batches of brownies. I had two identical Dutch ovens and round cake pans. I built two fires as alike as I could make them out of limb wood from the same tree. I mixed a double batch of brownie batter, and split it between the two pans. Cooked for equal lengths of time, one batch was perfect brownies and the other was so black and hard that we used it to play Frisbee on the meadow. Ah, well, you can't win them all.

When I got to Rock Creek, the best thing I learned about was five-gallon square tins. When you put handles on them, they make perfect water buckets. They fit right down in your pack boxes so they are easy to pack along, weighing very little and taking up no room at all. They can also be heated on the stove for wash water, and when they eventually wear out along the bottom, you can turn them on their sides and use them for ovens. Seriously, just lay one flat on your steel stove top and close the open end with foil. They will bake roasts, pies and cakes just like your oven at home. You should see the looks on the dudes' faces when after a layover day in the wilderness, you feed them prime rib for dinner.

Now most of the actual cooking stories you hear will involve food disasters. Every cook seems to have a few mistakes hanging over her like a dark cloud from the past. Mine was the time the creamed tuna got scorched. It was on a huge Sierra Club trip with 117 people. That much scorched tuna really stinks. According to Tommy Jefferson he could smell it three miles from camp and prayed all the way in that it wasn't OUR dinner.

Marge London was famous for the time she put an unopened can of brown bread in with a ham she was baking. It exploded and blew the ham clear to the other side of the camp. I remember a first year cook who mixed up two different sets of directions for reconstituting dried scalloped potatoes. The result was a large pot full of thin cream with some chunks of potato floating in it. She just served it before the salad and told the guests that it was potato soup. Another beginner made a potentially much more serious mistake. She mistook the chlorinated lime for flour and used it in the stew. Fortunately, it smelled so bad no one would touch it. Wes, one of the Rock Creek packers, tells a story about working with a cook who had her own horse that she let hang in close to her kitchen. One morning she whipped up the eggs for scrambling and left the bowl on the edge of the table. Her pet pony backed up to the table and let fly with something liquid and green. Wes says it missed the eggs by fractions of an inch, but when the cook went ahead and fried those eggs up, nobody much seemed to want them for breakfast. Though no one ever forgets them, those kinds of accidents are few and far between. Mostly pack cooks produce miracles on a regular basis.

One good trick is to never tell the guests what's for dinner that night. That way if things go wrong and you have to figure out something else to serve, they never know. The best trick of all in this business is to wait and cook anything new or tricky on a layover day while the guests and packers are out of camp. Then if it doesn't work out, you throw it in the bushes and fix a different dish. The only problem with these approaches is that when you have to figure out something else to do and you come up with something absolutely brilliant, nobody ever compliments your genius because they never knew you were in trouble in the first place. Guess it's better that way. Good luck with your camp cooking, and maybe someday I'll get to sample some of your work around the campfire.

AN OLD COOK MEETS A NEW OUTFIT

One spring this big tall veterinarian asked me about working for his pack outfit that summer. The next time I saw him I asked about the job. Apparently forgetting that he had asked me first, he looked me right in my forty-some face and said, "Rock Creek Pack Trains doesn't hire any OLD pack cooks. They're all too dirty and mean." I looked him right in the eye and allowed as how I might be old, dirty, and mean, but I was also one of the best pack cooks he was ever likely to meet. The next day his father, the big boss, called me and offered me work.

I was still working part-time for another outfit that summer, but somehow coming to Rock Creek felt a lot like coming home. The stock, the equipment, and the crew all reminded me of Mt. Whitney Pack Trains, an outfit a little farther to the south where I had first learned to pack and cook. Nobody there made speeches about what all this packing stuff meant, but if they had it would have been something like: "Care for the people. Care for the stock. Care for the land." These were priorities I understood, and I got the feeling Rock Creek Pack did, too.

The head of the crew for this first trip was Phil, an old-time packer, side whiskers and all. The only thing he knew better than packing and stock was the great range of mountains we traveled through. Our lady wrangler, Jamie, was a born hand who knew every inch of every head of stock in the outfit. The only thing she loved more than those horses and mules was our head packer. Our other packer was a wild kid named Kevin who probably loved the packing life but loved whiskey and "sierra sparrows" even more.

This trip was a seven day run from Rock Creek to Mammoth, a piece of country I'd been wanting to see for a mighty long time. Since Rock Creek makes this trip at least once every week, nowadays, I just call it "The Mammoth Shuttle" like everyone else at the outfit. But that first time heading in it was so pretty it like to broke my heart- Little Lakes Valley, a picture postcard come to life; up and up the sandy switchbacks; tip-toeing around above Ruby Lake and under overhanging rock; the desolate high lonesome of Mono Pass; the white slabs of Mono Rock towering over Bench Camp...

Bench Camp was our first and most enlightening stop on this sojourn into the wilderness. Our equipment included kitchen boxes and a great stove designed by none other than our head packer, a talented guy. It was a big step up from where I had been working. Setting to work on dinner I really appreciated the organization of this new outfit. While I worked I watched our dudes and dudettes getting adjusted to the wilderness. There was one "sierra sparrow" along. She was 18, alone, cute, and pining for the handsome packer she had met the year before. Our young packer already had his eyes and his hopes pinned on her. Unfortunately for him she couldn't see past her romantic dream of last year's hero.

Things began to go rapidly downhill for our wild, young cowboy. Hunkered down by the campfire, one of older guest started to put a fair sized dent in a fifth of whiskey. He invited the kid to join him. It was first night out so I figured they'd take it easy. Nobody likes to run dry part way through a trip. Boy howdy, was I wrong. These guys drank that fifth, another fifth of whiskey, and then they started on a fifth of tequila. They were telling stories and laughing fit to be tied. Finally, they both stood up and announced that they were going off in the woods for a knife throwing contest. It sounded to me like it could be pretty fatal. Lucky for our young packer, he only staggered about 15 feet before he passed out and fell face down in the rocks instead. Looked like it hurt, but it was probably the safer of his two options. We checked to see if he was dead, and finding him still alive, we just left him lay.

Dinner was served and clean-up taken care of. The head packer and the wrangler told stories around the campfire. Tired guests and crew wandered off to bed. A rare night rain began to fall. The young packer crawled off to beg a corner of someone's tent to sleep in. Snuggled down in my bedroll under the kitchen tarp, I watched the embers of the fire wink out in the rain. So this was the packing life with Rock Creek, I thought.

I drifted off to sleep. Late in the night something big and black moved through the darkness and into camp. It carefully snaked its head under the pack tarp covering our supplies. Knowing it must be a bear, I grabbed my flashlight and some rocks. Squishing through the cold mud in my bare feet, I moved toward our unwelcome visitor. I don't know about you guys, but facing a bear in the dark sorta makes my mouth go dry. The dark shape jerked up out of the food boxes and loomed over me. I'da likely soiled my dainties right then and there, but in the beam from my light I suddenly caught sight of two long ears. It wasn't a bear, just a damn kitchen-raiding mule. Smeared with pieces of apple clear up to his eyeballs, he grabbed one last bite and thundered off into the night. When I finally stopped laughing, I covered up what was left of my produce and headed back to bed. Yeah, this working for Rock Creek was going to be pretty interesting.

WRECK!

In many stories about the packing game in the High Sierra you will hear the term "wreck". Now a wreck is pretty much what it sounds like, one or more pack mules tangled in their ropes or down. For those of you who worry about getting in trouble with your riding horse while strolling down a country road, picture packing this way. First off, you aren't on a bomb-proof dude horse. Part of your job as a packer, cook or wrangler is to improve the general outlook of any riding animal that is not yet suitable for the average guest. That animal might be young and foolish, old and snakey, or just new to the rocky parts of the world. The footing under this not-so-faithful steed may be a nice, soft meadow, but more likely it is a narrow, rocky trail down a breathtaking cliff, a deep treacherous stream crossing, a bog hole hidden in a pleasant spot of green, or a swinging suspension bridge over a roaring river. Of course, you and your horse aren't out there alone. You are also leading a string of pack mules or deadheading a bunch of empty riding animals. Strings average five mules but can range from one to fifteen head. The most I have ever dragged was taking ten empty horses from Mineral King across the Sierra to Cottonwood, 60 miles in two days. If you think controlling one equine is difficult, imagine controlling the packer's average number of six. Since you usually have five mules tied together, one mule in trouble can take down your whole string. Something as simple as a mule stepping over his lead rope can result in dead or injured mules, shattered equipment, and wounded packers.

The best way to deal with wrecks is to prevent them. Well, that's obvious, but how do you do it? First, your equipment should be properly adjusted and your loads well balanced. Your animals should be healthy, sound and well shod. Having experienced pack mules can make a huge difference. And, always carry a knife.

The order you string your mule up in is also a deciding factor in how your day is going to go. The mule that hates to have an animal behind him or one that kicks should always be your tail mule. An animal that drags, is slow, or tends to leave the trail should be first so you can hand lead him. Your solid, good-minded animals go in the middle. New green mules should be tied in behind a big quiet older mule that can provide security when they panic and hold them steady if they try to run. I remember one trip where I had two big stout mules that always pestered the mules around them in the string and caused a fair number of wrecks along the way. Sidney liked to cock a hind leg at the mule behind him until it pulled back enough that it had no more slack. Then he could jump forward and jerk that mule down in the rocks. Turnip had a similar trick but it involved nipping the mule ahead of him until it crowded the mule in front of it. Turnip would do this just as they were coming into a switchback. When the other animal jumped forward above the turn, Turnip would step back on the lower part and stretch the rope between them across the turn. That let Turnip pull the other animal off the trail and cause a wreck. After one day of trying to straighten out the messes they caused, I figured out that if I put them together they would just annoy each other and let the rest of the mules alone. Worked pretty good. We just went on down the trail with Sidney kicking Turnip and Turnip biting Sidney, but they were both so big and strong that neither one could knock the other down.

As I said before, ALWAYS carry a knife. Always have it sharp and in easy reach. One time in my early years at Mt. Whitney I let the boss's yelling at me rattle me enough that I failed to take the time to get my knife. Heading up the trail I thought about going back for it, but couldn't face the fact that it would convince Tommy that I was an idiot. I consoled myself with the fact that I was only leading half a dozen empty saddle horses and didn't have to worry about loads. Also, we were just jumping over the hill from Horseshoe Meadows to the pasture at the head of Little Cottonwood, only about an hour's ride. No more than half an hour later several of the empty horses I was leading got tangled up in a grove of small pine trees. One big gray horse ended up with his lead rope wrapped around several small trees, while the horse behind spooked around another group of trees. The horse in front tried to keep going. The horse in back pulled back on the rope tied around the gray's neck. Stretched out tight, he sank to the ground slowly strangling to death. With no knife to cut the ropes, I tried frantically to unbuckle his halter. With several thousand pounds of horses pulling on it, the halter was impossible to undo. As I struggled with the strap, the horse's breathing became more desperate and his eyes rolled back in his head. I knew I was going to lose him. But just then Sam Livermore rode up and saved us. Bailing off his horse and whipping out his knife, he cut the gray's ropes. Sam was just a tall blonde kid in his first few years of packing, but even he knew enough to never get caught without his knife. I should have been real embarrassed by pulling a gunsel trick like that, but I was so glad to see him that I never even thought about feeling bad. The gray horse soon recovered, and for the rest of my life I never went anywhere without a knife in my pocket.

The first real wreck I ever saw was on New Army Pass on a long switchback high on a talus slope. I was riding with the guests at the bottom of the slope and we all got a heck of a view of the whole wreck. High above us were the packer (Ray Delea-The Pygmy Packer) his horse, and a string of five mules. Suddenly his middle mule pulled back and stopped the whole string. Just as Ray swung off his horse, the mule slowly sat down like a dog. Then he slowly leaned back and rolled off the trail. Ray whipped out his knife and scrambled to cut the ropes connecting the animals to each other. Too late. The down mule took the other four mules off the trail with him. Horrified, we all watched in silence as the mules rolled and bounced down through the steep jumble of broken rocks. The pack loads came apart and scattered dunnage all down the mountain. When the mules finally stopped rolling, they just lay there looking like scattered, broken toys. Right now, I could stretch this story out by telling all about how it felt to see this and think they were all dead, but the simple fact is that all five of the mules were okay. With the help of the other packers who walked down from where they'd left their strings on top of the pass, Ray got the shaken animals on their feet and back onto the trail. It took about an hour for them to gather up all the stuff scattered in the rocks and repack it. Then we headed on up the trail.

Later I got a chance to look the mules over up close. Except for some cuts and scrapes, they were fine. I asked one of the more experienced hands how that was possible. He pointed out that they were carrying dunnage loads, and all the bedrolls and duffle bags had both protected them from the rocks and cushioned their fall. As terrifying as this wreck looked, the hardest part for me was talking the dudes into riding up the talus after watching the mules come bouncing down it.

Another impressive wreck back in the Mt. Whitney days happened on the bridge at the lower end of Paiute Creek. We came in over Paiute Pass out of North Lake above Bishop. On our second day we followed Paiute Creek down to where it joined the John Muir Trail and the San Joaquin River. That was a pretty rough trail and a big ol' creek. We had both heard the story how another outfit drowned an entire string of mules on the upper, smaller part of that creek. So we started out being glad that the lower part where we would cross it had a bridge. My packer on this trip was Sam's older brother, Norrie Livermore, who was all of 17 years old. In those days packers started young, and at this time Norrie was an experienced hand working his third season in the high lonesome. He was not only packing an 18 day trip by himself, but was working a string of five grass green mules. Actually they had been worked some, because by this time only one of them still needed to be blind-folded and have a leg tied up to get packed. Of course none of them had ever seen a bridge before. So on this second day of the trip our arrival at the Paiute Creek crossing was faced with a certain amount of trepidation. It has a big steel bridge, eight feet wide, about 40 feet long, and maybe 20 feet in the air. Fortunately, our guests had hiked on ahead and were not there for the "great bridge crossing".

Norrie sent me to ride across first so I would be in the clear if anything went wrong. On the far side I whipped out my camera and took a quick shot of the string starting across the bridge. Norrie and the first two mules were on the bridge and lookin' good. I glanced down to drop the camera in my bag and by the time I looked back up everything had gone to hell. Norrie, his horse, and the first mule were still comin'. The last two mules had their feet planted at the edge of the bridge and were pulling back for all they were worth. The two middle mules were terror-stricken and were bucking and thrashing out on the middle of the bridge. At this point the bridge looked a whole lot narrower than it had just a few minutes before. First one mule and then the other lost their footing, fell on the bridge, and lay stranded high above the river, stretched out between the front and back mules and pinned by the weight of their pack loads. My first thought was that there was no way to get them up and off the bridge without dumping them off that long drop to the thundering water below. But Norrie quickly separated the mules. The mules that were still on their feet swiftly left the vicinity of the bridge. With the help of his saddle horse, Norrie got the two down mules up on their feet. They also got the heck off that mule eatin' bridge. I was shaking with relief when I knew that all of us (the animals, people and packs) were safe on solid ground. It had been the kind of situation where you coulda lost the whole string.

It took the grim look on Norrie's face to point out that while we were all safe, we were also on the wrong side of the bridge. It was obvious that by now the mules were much less fond of this bridge than back when we started. There was no chance of leading them across as a string. Norrie thought they might go across pulled one at a time by his horse. He was riding his own big stout mare, Cindy, and she should have been able to move the mules. Not a chance. They had all learned pretty fast that if you dug in all four feet right at the edge of the bridge, you could stop the lead horse dead in her tracks. You lovers of equines are going to hate this part, but at this point it became my job to give the mules what the old timers called "a taste of chain soup". A proper mule rope has about a foot of chain at one end, and in situations like this you swing the rope and whack the mule across the butt with the chain part. Mules, even green ones, are more practical-minded than horses. Faced by this kind of pressure many horses might go nuts and do something fatal like jumping off the bridge, but a mule thinks differently. A mule's thoughts go more like this, "I ain't going across that bridge and you can't make me. My feet are on solid dirt and that's where they're stayin'! Drag all you want, I'm stayin'….OUCH! What the heck was that? …Like I said I ain't going and…OUCH!! My butt is startin' to hurt over here. Maybe I would feel better someplace else like over to the other side of this thing. OUCH! Yep, I really want to be on the other side of this danged bridge. Maybe I could just follow this nice, old horse across. Here I go. Yup, I always knew I'd rather be over here."

So one at a time with Norrie and his horse pulling and me providing the encouragement, we eventually got all five mules to the other side of the bridge. Back on solid ground, Norrie quietly reassured the shaken mules and tied them back together into a string. Safely strung together they proceeded on up the San Joaquin River into Kings Canyon National Park. Since we were headed for Evolution Valley and neither of us had been there before, I dug my map out of my saddle bags as we rode along. I took a good look at the trail ahead of us. Norrie asked me what it looked like. Taking a deep breath, I allowed as how we were going to just wind along the river for quite a spell. He felt as how that would be a relief. Then I told him we would switchback up the east wall, which didn't look too steep. And then we would come to our camp site in a high valley hung up on the side of the canyon. He seemed to think we could probably do okay on that. I hesitated a while and hemmed and hawed, but I finally told him that the only problem appeared to be that there were two more bridges between us and camp. But that's another story for another campfire.

Oh, and about that picture I took just at the start of things. I figured it would turn out to be pretty spectacular, showing things just before the wreck or maybe even catching the start of the action. Guess I was a better cook than photographer because it turned out to be a fairly blurry shot of my horse's ears.

MORE WRECKS AND NEAR WRECKS

Many things in the High Sierra will stick in your memory forever: the beauty of the high lonesome, the friendship, humor, and bravery of the crew members you work with, the fascinating characters that you meet as guests, and the love and loyalty of your animals. Also indelibly printed on your mind are those moments when everything blew apart and lives hung on your next action. Just being the old fat camp cook, most of the heroics during these wrecks fell to someone other than myself, usually the packer.

The Eastern Sierra is unfortunately full of stories about wrecks, some of them tragic. Everyone has heard the story about an entire string of animals being caught in the water near the drift fence on Paiute Creek and being swept to their deaths. Another time a section of trail gave away along the lower part of Fish Creek and dumped seven or eight head down a cliff. One part of Duk Lake where the shore swings in close under the much higher trail, is called Dead Mule Bay. Guess I don't have to explain the reason for the name. So far I have been real lucky. I've been there when stock has been hurt, and I have friends who have lost animals, but so far I haven't been in a wreck where we killed one. I hope my luck holds because I have lost horses in my life outside the mountains and I didn't much like it. Hope saying this doesn't jinx me for next summer.

Funny thing about wrecks is that some packers like to tell stories about them and others don't. Some guys will tell hair-raising wreck stories at the drop of a hat. I guess that's because they're exciting and make the hands involved sound pretty western. Some others, especially old timers, never talk about wrecks. It's kinda like that by talking about them you might cause one to happen. And, you know, most of us would be perfectly happy if we never saw another wreck, let alone had one. All that said, I guess I'd better get busy and tell some of these hair-raising tales.

Now sometimes you have wrecks, and other times you have near wrecks. Those are the ones where you get into a potentially disastrous situation, and somehow get out of it no worse for wear. Once many years ago when the Mt. Whitney trail was open to stock, I was leading a group of guests on horseback over Trail Crest. This is the pass that leads to Mt. Whitney, is 13,777 feet in elevation, and is a window. Now a window is a spot where the mountainside drops off on both sides of the trail. In this case it dropped several hundred feet on the west side and a sheer thousand feet to the east. It sorta clashes with the western "ambiance" of this story, but right there we met a fighter jet. He roared up the east side and broke the sound barrier right in our faces. He was so close that I could see that his helmet was red and had lettering across the front. You and I both know that a horse's most common response to terror is to shy and run. Unfortunately there was no place to go but down. And you had to be able to fly to do that. Fortunately the boom the plane made was so startling that all the horses just went spraddle legged and froze. In a second the plane was gone. Aside from having the bejaybers scared out of us, we were all fine. That's what I call a near wreck. Funny, but just thinking about it still makes my heart pound.

Another near wreck was years later working for Rock Creek. It was the first time I came down Taboose Pass. Now our boss, Craig London, had told us that we shouldn't feel too bad if we killed something up there because it was that bad a trail. Just the kind of thing you wanted to hear when facing unknown country. I was leading five big, stout mules. We had already been together fifteen pretty tough days on this trip so I had a lot of faith in those long-earred guys. In the first mile or so we were working our way down through some pretty rough talus when the trail just flat disappeared. I looked all around but there was no trail, just piles of shattered boulders in every direction. It seemed our best bet was to work our way over to the right. Before too long I found that my horse and I were on one side of a huge flat-topped, circular boulder and my mules were about eight feet away on the other side looking real worried. Normally I would have backed my horse up through the talus to the mules and started over. Unfortunately, Able, my little palomino appy had recently gone blind in one eye and was afraid to back up. So the mules needed to get to me. To do that, the mules would have to back up to the left and work their way through the talus around the boulder. My rope was useless to me. Tugging on the lead rope would just pull them into the impassable boulder. Hoping that there was some kind of bond between me and them old mules, I started asking them to come to me. I said, "Hey, Rhonda, come on over here old girl. Come to the left. That's a girl." And by golly, she worked her way around the rock until she was standing next to me. While she was working around, I talked to the rest of them, "Come on Art. You can do it. Easy Sidney, just keep comin'. Okay, Turnip, now you. Come on little tail mule, you too." And pretty soon we were all safe and together. Damn, I loved those mules. In another hundred yards or so we found the rest of the trail. Guess Craig was wrong and it was only a near wreck and we weren't going to lose anyone that day.

Like I said before, I've never been in a wreck where we lost an animal, but sometimes it seems like no matter how hard you try, things just go from bad to worse. One day not too many years back, I was working a trip with a group of hikers. My packers were Little Phil, kind, quiet and competent, and Chris, one of the boys from Texas. They were both real hands or we would never have made it through that day. We were coming down the Muir between Silver Pass and the upper end of Cascade Valley. The boys each had a string, but I was just riding along enjoying the scenery. It was comin' on to storm so we hoped to get down off the high part before it got too wet. When the trail crossed the outlet of Squaw Lake, the boys let the mules stop to drink. The water there was only about a foot deep, but old Thelma, one of Chris's mules, got in trouble. Her hind legs just sorta folded up and she went down. Chris separated her from the other mules and then gave getting her up a try. She struggled up, lost her balance and fell into deeper water. I was still up on my mule, holding Phil's stock as he waded in to help Chris. By then the storm had settled in and it was raining, but everyone was too wet to notice.

In the freezing lake water, Chris and Phil struggled to take off Thelma's pack load and drag it to the shore. Then they tried to get her up. Again, she made the try, lost her balance, and flipped over into ever deeper water. This time the boys took off her saddle and pad and tried again. If she didn't make it this time, it was starting to look like we might lose her. The cold water and exhaustion were taking their toll and her struggles were obviously getting weaker. With both of the guys pulling on her, Thelma made a valiant, final effort and came surging out of the water. For a moment I thought we had made it. Then she flipped over backwards and landed in the damnedest position I've ever seen. Sticking out of the lake was a tiny island. On top of the island was a big, split-topped rock. Upside down, in the split, lay Thelma. She had all four feet in the air, but her head was hanging down like she was give out. The boys waded in one more time and picking up the ropes pulled with all their might. They were hoping to roll her sideways over the rock, but their pulls didn't even budge her considerable weight. The split in the rock was too deep for them to roll her out that way. Thinking that a little mule power might help, I rode my mule, Abby, into the water to help pull. Just as I took one of the ropes from Phil, I suddenly remembered Craig rescuing Jasper from a similar fix. He had gotten him out by pulling the rope straight down the mule's middle between his hind legs. We all changed the angles we were pulling. Knowing it was probably our last chance to save her, we all pulled straight down her middle. Then Thelma rolled right up and out of that rock like your fat Uncle George being helped out of his recliner. She landed on her feet and managed a shaky walk to dry land.

Poor old Thelma was shaking with the cold. The boys started resaddling her. Everything was real wet, real cold, and real heavy from all the lake water the equipment had soaked up. I remember watching the water run off the corners of the saddle pad like a faucet turned full on. The storm intensified and you could hear the thunder and lightening moving our way. Our guest hikers came by just about then, a very sweet group of ladies from New England. They laughed about beating us to camp and hurried on their way. It was obvious that they had no idea what was going on. Sometimes it's just as well if the guests don't know about the wrecks.

Before too much longer we were back on the trail, headed for camp, and looking forward to a warm campfire and a dry bed. We got just about 300 yards before we were in trouble again. I was riding lead so my Abby mule and I were the first to come to a huge boulder in the trail. Shining wet from the rain, it completely blocked the trail. The sidehill was too steep to drop off and work around it. The only possibility was to scramble up the pile of loose gravel that had gathered behind the rock, squeeze between the top of the boulder and the hillside, then slide down onto the trail on the other side. Pointing poor little

Abby that way, I took a deep breath and kicked her in the sides. She clawed her way up, slipped through and slid back down onto the trail on the far side. Whew! We were through.

Of course now all we had to do was get two packers, their horses and two strings of mules up around the same spot. Most of the mules and their loads were way bigger than Abby and I, so nothing guaranteed that we could get them through. It was pretty easy to tell that taking the animals through one at a time was our only hope. I took Abby about 50 feet down the trail and tied her to a small tree. Then I came back to take hold of whatever animals the guys got over the boulder. First Phil brought his horse over and I tied it down with Abby. Phil unstrung his mules and got the first one up and over the boulder. As I reached up to take the lead, I realized that it was Rio, not exactly my favorite mule. A huge bay draft cross, he had always gotten his own way by running over me or dragging me until he got where he wanted to be. Right now all I had to do was hold him quiet while the boys worked the other mules over the boulder and tied them in behind him. With each additional mule, we moved forward far enough to give the guys room to work. The storm worsened to the point I could hardly see and the lightening seemed to be all around us. But the boys just kept working and it started to look like we were going to get it done.

So the bunch on the hillside looked like this: Abby and Phil's horse tied to a tree. Then one short cook holding one really big mule. Then there were four more mules strung on to Rio, Chris's loose horse, and the first three mules of Chris's string. Behind that were Phil and Chris working the next-to-the-last mule around the rock. As she scrambled up to the high point, she sorta folded up in back and jammed down between the boulder and the hillside. It was Thelma again and I figure she was just too exhausted from her wreck in the lake to struggle past this last barrier. Chris had to unpack her to get her up and over the rock. While he was doing that, the storm zeroed in on us and lightening was striking really close. I kept looking at Rio's big scared eyes. If he blew up, there wasn't any place for us to go. I figured the most likely result would be that he would trample me, run into the horse ahead of me, then dump himself and the rest of the string off the side. Just as I was thinking how fatal that might be for all of us, my hair stood on end and all the air around us made hissing, crackling noises. Suddenly everything turned bright white and there was a boom so loud that you felt it more than you heard it. Rio and the entire string levitated about a foot in the air, but to my amazement they came back down right in the same place. They were so spooked that they just stood right there and shook. Rio stood his ground and the rest of the mules stayed because he did. That was the first time I ever worked with Rio that he didn't try to kill me. Changed my feelings about him considerable.

After we survived that near miss by the lightening, things started to get a bit easier. Chris and Phil got Thelma over the rock and repacked. Then they got the last mule across and got everybody strung back together. Seemed like after all of this, we should have been in the clear for the rest of the day. It didn't seem fair, but the rest of the day was one minor annoyance after another. One hundred yards down the trail from the boulder, Chris realized that he had failed to repack his own fishing rod on Thelma. On foot Chris had to climb back up and get it. At the bottom of the canyon Fish Creek was running so high that after we got the stock across, the boys had to ride back across the creek to string a safety rope so our hikers could cross without being swept away. Then we had to find a camp in the storm and gathering dark. Not always easy to find a spot 100 feet from water, 100 feet from the trail, and flat enough for a camp. The place we did find was marginal at best. After we got unpacked and set up, we discovered that there was a little hidden stream too close for us to be legal. We try real hard to abide by the rules, but sometimes you just have to say the heck with it. Maybe it wasn't really a creek, just runoff from the storm?

A little later, I was starting dinner while Phil rode out to bring in firewood. Poor Chris was up the hill trying to dig a privy in a pile of rock. I was pretty damn tired and I knew the boys had to be way past exhausted. After dinner I was working on the dishes and wondering why anyone in their right mind would do this kind of work. About then our guests gathered at the camp fire and began to sing. They were singing a song in Latin and covering all the parts. Dang, that was pretty. Sounded like a choir in a monastery somewhere. It made me feel a whole lot better than I had just a few minutes before. About then Phil scrambled over next to me and apparently in a panic said, "Listen to that! They must be nuns. Nobody sings like that but nuns. Oh, no. They're nuns, and I've been cussing and telling rowdy stories in front of them." I tried to explain that they were just a nice group of middle-aged professional ladies from the Boston area who could sing real pretty. Guess he didn't believe me because he was real careful of his language for the rest of the trip, even on the last day when his horse went over on him and busted his shoulder. And to this day whenever someone mentions the wrecks we had on this trip, Phil says, "Yeah, that was on that trip with the nuns."

Well, that's about all the wrecks I can talk about at one time. I'll have to save the rest for another story or another campfire.

LOOKING BACK, LOOSE HERDING, AND MORE WRECKS

If you want to surprise a packer on the trail, just step out in front of him right in the middle of the trail. Chances are 90 out of 100 that he will be riding looking back, and he won't even know you are there until his horse spooks. A good packer spends most of his time watching his string. If someone shows you a picture of a packer leading a string and he is staring soulfully forward out across the high lonesome, I can guarantee that he is either a gunsel or he was posing for the photographer.

Why does a packer travel this way? Well, as I might have mentioned in some other stories about wrecks, the best thing to do about mule wrecks is not to have them. Some of the preventatives include carrying a knife, having strong healthy well-shod mules, and making balanced loads that will ride. One reason for riding looking back is to see that your loads are riding. Since a difference of only a pound or two in your side loads can pull your load off, it's a good idea to watch them. When you pack up, be sure to tuck your tarp in behind the sawbucks since that will allow you to see if your load starts to slip. If the red X made by the fork of the sawbuck isn't right in the middle, you are in trouble. Though it doesn't look real fancy, the best thing to do when the load slips is to stop, pull the load straight, and slide a piece of rock under the lash rope on the light side. In the old days, the real packers called that "packin' granite" and looked with contempt on anyone who had to do that because it meant that they hadn't gotten their loads right in the first place. Now days everyone does it. In fact at Reds Meadows they use a method they call "Big rock, little rock". They don't bother to straighten the load. They just put a heavy rock on the light side and stick a small rock in their pocket. As they ride along, the big rock gradually pulls the load over. When it gets straight, they put the little rock on the other side to keep it from going any farther.

The more important reason for looking back is that a pack "train" is called that because it moves much like a railroad train. Often your lead mule starts moving when you pull him. The second mule doesn't move until the front mule jerks on his lead rope which starts the second mule but may stop the first mule. Thus the mules get going by a series of jerks, starts, and stops, the same way a train of freight cars starts out of a railroad yard. Teaching your mules to start out on your whistle can prevent a lot of this. Since one of my many flaws is the inability to whistle, I just get my mules to start moving when I yell "Hut!" at them. If you're not watching them at this point, you may have your first wreck of the day right there in the station yard which could be mighty embarrassing.

So now you are leading your string along through the beautiful High Sierra and you come to your first rough spot on the trail. Let's say you have to jump down three big ol' rocks in a row. First, you slow up at the top so your mules can get some slack in their ropes. Now you ride your horse down the first rock while you play out the first mule's lead rope so you don't pull him down on top of you. Slow your horse while you pull the lead mule down the first rock. Stop the mule then ride your horse down the second rock. Now stop your horse, and pull the mules so the first and second mules each do one rock. Keep doing the stop and start until the tail mule reaches the bottom of the last rock. This requires that you and your horse are doing stop and starts long after you reach level ground. Needless to say you will be looking back most of the time. During those few moments when you must look forward to guide your horse, you should have most of you concentration on the slack in your lead rope so you can feel where your mules are. Every time you go up a rough spot, go down one, or go around a switchback, you get to repeat this maneuver. After all this stop and start stuff in the rocks, you really look forward to nice open meadows in hopes you will get a chance to just ride along without any hassle. Unfortunately, when you do get to that meadow, the mules all spread out sideways to get a snack. They put their heads down to eat, step over their lead ropes, kick the mule behind them catching their hind leg over that mule's rope, and soon you have a big wreck right out there in that nice flat meadow. Before long you start looking forward to a nice, narrow, rough section of rocky trail that will keep your string lined out.

In the old days packers handled the really rough sections of trail by loose herding. To do that, you untie each animal from the one in front of it. Then you fasten the lead ropes on top of each mule's pack. One packer takes the lead in hopes that the stock will follow him. Each remaining packer herds the stock in front of him. The equipment he uses is a pocket full of rocks and a loud voice. Yelling and a few well thrown rocks keep the mules from bunching up on the corners or turning back. Loose herding is no longer allowed in much of the Sierra. You can only use it in areas where being strung together would be life threatening for your mules. A good example of such a place was the 99 switchbacks on the Whitney trail. The switchbacks were so short that a string of five would have been on three different switchbacks at the same time. If they were strung together, they would have been real likely to pull each other off the trail. Not a good idea since the trail was on a cliff with a drop of up to

1000 feet under it. Even loose herding was dangerous there. In fact it was so narrow and steep that the forest service had signs dictating which time of day you were allowed to go which direction on the trail. That was to prevent meetings where it was impossible to pass or turn back. One time back in 1967, Tom Jefferson was taking a resupply over that trail when he met a group that was traveling against the time rules. He was loose herding a string of very green mules and was accompanied by his 12 year old daughter Kathy. Kathy was riding in the behind the string and the mules in front of her panicked and turned back on her. Her horse was trapped by the panicked mules and shoved off the cliff. As her horse went over, Kathy was still in the saddle. Tom saw what was happening, leaped off his horse, and reached Kathy just as her waist disappeared below the edge of the trail. With that unbelievable strength that often comes to a parent whose child is in mortal danger, Tom grabbed her waist and jerked her straight up and over the trail to land on top of one of the pack mules' load. Luckily she then slid off the mule and landed safe and sound on the inside of the trail. Her horse fell, slid and bounced over 400 feet to a snow bank at the bottom of the cliff. Kathy walked down the trail while Tommy and Norie got the rest of the mules over the top of the pass and strung back together. While Norie took the string on to Crabtree Meadows, Tommy came back and he and Kathy worked their way down to where her mare had fallen. To everyone's surprise, they found Kathy's mare alive at the base of the cliff. She had survived the fall though she never completely recovered from her injuries.

More recently I did some loose herding over Glenn Pass. Glenn is a big ol' pass. The top is around 13,000 feet and has a 30 foot knife edge where you can look straight down on either side of you. Strangely enough that scary ol' part isn't where most of the wrecks happen. When you get into the longer switchbacks on the south side, the stock starts getting confused by the animals moving the opposite direction below them. The first time I rode my Abby mule over Glenn, things got a little western. On the south side, Turnip got a whole bunch of loose mules tangled up on a switchback. I was the next hand behind them so it was my job to go down and straighten them out. I jumped off Abby, and tying her reins up to the saddlehorn, I left her to come down the trail by herself. I cut a switchback on foot and got Turnip and his buddies turned around and headed safely down the trail. Walking back up the trail to retrieve my mule, I was less than pleased to see her standing on the corner of a switchback staring at some of our riders below us. Like all mules her number one goal was to catch up with the horses. It didn't occur to her that the best way to do that was to turn right on the trail, go a ways and then turn left to get where they were. Instead she was standing on a very steep corner contemplating jumping off. Hoping she would wait until I got to her, I hurried up the trail as fast as my fat, little legs would carry me. When I was still about ten feet from her, the packer behind us got into the act. Not too experienced with loose herding, he saw her standing there and pegged her in the side of the head with a rock. Taking that as a sign that she was in the wrong spot, Abby bailed right off that corner. She slid, wallowed, buck jumped, and fought her way down about 200 feet of real steep hillside without ever losing her footing. My boss, Dr. London, was ahead of us and caught her when she reached the trail. I scrambled downhill to where the doctor and the mule were waiting for me. Dr. London was looking back up the hill at Abby's tracks, shaking his head, and laughing. He handed me her reins and said, "My, that sure is an ath-e-letic mule." I wasn't real sure if I thought it was all that funny. No sense of humor, I guess.

Sense of humor or not, sometimes wrecks are just plain funny. Once after a long snowy winter, there was still heavy snow on the high passes even in late August. Silver Pass is less than 12,000 feet, and one of the easier passes on the John Muir Trail. But on the year in question we were one of the first stock parties to cross it and that was on August 23rd. The entire top was under about ten feet of hard packed snow. If you tried to slide down the snow where the regular trail was, it would drop you neatly off a cliff and into a lake. So the thing to do was to cross the deepest part of the snow and drop off the cornice. Then all you had to do was slide to the bottom of the snow which left you safely at the end of the rocky hillside. We separated the animals from the strings like any other loose herding. Then we led them a couple at a time out to the lip of the cornice. There we either led or pushed them down the hill. Being more than a little overconfident of the treads on my new riding shoes, I led my mule Abby and two pack mules, Maxine and Annie, out to the drop. I was so sure of myself that I was leading Abby by her reins instead of by her lead rope like I was supposed to be doing. Just over the edge I slipped and went whizzing down the hill. If I'd had the lead rope, I could have held on and stopped myself. But I knew that trying to stop myself with Abby's reins would tear up her mouth and she was way too good a mule to treat that way. So I threw the reins back at her and let myself slide all the way to the bottom. The slope leveled out a little before I got all the way to the rocks at the bottom, so I landed with no damage to anything but my pride. One of the packers still up top caught my mules and sent them down to me. My boss, Craig London, was already at the bottom of the hill with most of the guests. He was laughing so hard it put me in mind of one of the mules braying. He just kept saying as how I looked like a real fool and all those guests had cameras and videos and surely had lots of pictures of my moment of shame. I just hung my head and felt bad until one after the other the guests all said that no, they hadn't gotten a picture. So I figured the laugh was on Craig. The rest of the day went fine except that my jeans were full of ice and froze my butt off for the remainder of the ride. It wasn't until the same trip the following year that I realized that the guests had just felt sorry for me and there really were pictures of me on Silver Pass. That was when the Campbells, a nice couple from Australia, gave me a great 8 x 10 photo of me going down the snow while Abby stood on the lip of the cornice with a look of amazement on her face. It had a caption on it that said "On your ass on Silver Pass". Even without much of a sense of humor, I thought that was funny as hell.

One other wreck that comes to mind was in northern Yosemite just north of Benson Lake. It was yet another Henkes trip and my packers were Craig London and Kent Dohnel. Kent was a really fine packer who spent a lot of time gentling some of the rank old mules. He had a quiet way and a kind voice. There were several big rank mules that wouldn't work for anyone but him. On this trip he was riding a black mustang named Blacky, and leading a string of five that included Maxine and Turnip. Blacky was a mustang that had been captured wild as an eight year old stallion and still wasn't real tame. Turnip was a big bay john who was often in the middle of one wreck or another. Maxine was a small brown molly with an attitude like permanent PMS. Eight hours a day she would walk down the trail kicking at the animal behind her. Fairly frequently she would catch her hind leg over the lead rope of the mule she was trying to kick. Instant wreck! So of course, that day near Benson Lake Maxine got her leg caught and she and Turnip got in one hell of a fight. Being behind Kent's string, I dropped my animals and ran around to the rocks beside the struggling mules. Whipping out my knife I climbed up on the rocks. I was just reaching for the main rope, when Craig started bellowing at me to get out of there. He distracted me just enough for me to miss the rope. Then the mules went after each other again and knocked me ass over teakettle off the rocks. Kent came in from the other side, and just then Blacky reverted to his past as a boss stallion and attacked the battling mules. Blacky's left foreleg slipped down between the tangled ropes. One rope slid up behind his elbow and began to cut into his skin. Enraged, he attacked the mules again. Every time he tried to pull away, the rope cut deeper into his leg and he attacked the mules yet again. Finally, Kent just started cutting every rope he came to until the animals were free. We still had to run Blacky off the mules. He was really pissed. When he found himself free on the trail, he just made a bid for his freedom. He took off running down the trail. Kent found him over two miles away and not real eager to return.

The next morning at Kerrick Canyon, Blacky's leg was all swollen up from the deep rope burn under his elbow. Kent led him down and stood him in the creek to take down the swelling. As I watched them, Kent was talking to that little black horse in his own quiet way. The cool stream was soothing Blacky's leg and Kent's voice was soothing his soul. And as I watched, Blacky dropped his forehead on Kent's chest, closed his eyes and sighed. I could almost see him deciding that wrecks and all, being a tame horse might be okay after all.

PACKING SCHOOL BEAR

Packing school is a seven day pack trip that is crewed by the boss, one experienced packer and one cook. The rest of the group is made up of first-year packers and cooks working for the outfit and guests who are interested in learning how to horse pack in the High Sierra. The trip makes frequent short moves as the green hands learn how to pack their loads. Being as I am the regular pack cook, I get to train the new cooks on how to survive in a backcountry kitchen. Hopefully, the rest of the group survives the learning period.

One of the pack cook's least favorite duties is to sleep in the kitchen in case a bear tries to raid the supplies. Normally the cook has to do this because the packer has to sleep on the picket line to safeguard the wrangle horses and keep the bears out of the equipment and grain. Even when there are two packers, it seems that they're both needed on the picket line. I've never quite understood that part, but far be it for me to question the packers' wisdom. So after a day of work that goes from 4:30 AM to well after dark, the cook gets to spread her bedroll in a spot close to the kitchen and the food boxes. And there she lies armed with a few rocks and sticks, a noisy pan, and a small flashlight that always seems to go out at the crucial moment.

This particular packing school started out over Mono Pass and camped our first night at Widowmaker Camp. On our way in we met another trip from our outfit which was headed for the front country. They had a sick mule that couldn't carry his load. Normally they would have split his load between their other animals, but they knew we were about to camp for several days at the camp they had just left. By the time we moved, we would be traveling light, so they left us part of his load. They left us one pack box, one lash rope, half a bag of grain, a sack of trash, a container of powdered red punch mix, and a head of cabbage. This happened years ago, but I still remember exactly what they left because the bear got to it first.

The outbound packers had put everything in the pack box then hoisted it up a pine tree on a lash rope. By the time we got there the bear had climbed the tree and smashed the box so that everything else fell out on the ground. The camp was a real sight. At one point was an empty grain sack. Next to it was a pile of bear scat just full of undigested grain. Then there was the remains of a black garbage sack and another pile of scat, this one about 80% foil. Bear's insides must be really tough. Next we found the empty plastic punch container. Next to it was, of course, another pile of bear droppings. This one was dyed bright red by the punch. The head of cabbage was just sitting untouched in the middle of camp. I've never been real fond of cabbage, but this was the first time I realized that not even a bear will eat that stuff.

After cleaning up the mess, we made camp, fixed dinner, and after washing up the dishes, prepared to settle in for the night. All the pack boxes were in a neat row, covered with tarps and booby trapped with pots and pans. Normally, the cook sleeps in the kitchen and guards the food. As I mentioned earlier, the packer sleeps on the picket line to guard the grain and saddles, but most importantly to make sure that neither of the wrangle horses gets in trouble on the picket line. As I watched all the packers gather up their bedrolls and head for the picket line, I realized that including the boss, the regular packer, and the new guys, there were going to be six packers guarding the picket line. Let's see…we know there is a bear here that will be in the kitchen as soon as the lights are out. We have one old cook all alone against the bear. And we have six brave packers guarding each other about 100 yards away. After due consideration, I headed over to discuss the situation with the boss. The result was a new packer named Chris assigned to the kitchen for the night.

Now, Chris was new to Rock Creek but he had three or so years working pack trips on the West Side under his belt. Being a bit sensitive about protecting his status as an experienced hand, he wasn't too happy with his new assignment. Kitchen work wasn't packin'. So muttering about "Chicken shit old women who are afraid of the dark", he rolled his bed out right against the side of the food boxes and went to sleep. Knowing we could expect the bear soon, I lay awake waiting. Right away I heard strange sounds in the kitchen, but it was just Chris snoring. After a while I heard other noises, and could smell the distinctive smell of wet dog and garbage that tells you that a black bear is nearby. Turning on my flashlight I could see her trying to slip her head under the pack tarp. She was right across a pack box from Chris. He was still snoring. I jumped up and made lots of noise, scaring her away. I walked over to the boxes to check and see if she got anything. Standing there next to Chris's bedroll, I realized that he was still asleep. So I kicked him a few times to make sure that he was awake to enjoy the evening's activities.

He came up out of the bedroll mad as a wet hen. I told him that a bear had been in the kitchen and only about two feet from his head. He told me that I was crazy. He also told me that I wouldn't know a bear if I sat on it. Then he said several other things probably not suitable for this story. He finished up by stating that I had made the whole thing up. While he was enlightening me as to my many flaws as a human being, I could hear the bear slipping back into camp. By the time he finished talking, she was right back where she started, just across the box from our irate packer. Looking Chris in the eye, I said, "I just want you to do one thing for me. Turn your head to the left and take a deep breath." Grudgingly, he did. He gagged. Then he looked back at me and whispered, "What is that God-awful smell?" I replied, "That's the bear and she's standing right next to you." Swinging his light around, he spotted her by the food boxes. After a lot of yelling and screaming, the bear left camp again.

Without any comment, I returned to my bedroll. Feeling sure that Chris would keep a close watch for the rest of the night, I snuggled down for a peaceful sleep. The few times that I woke during the night I could see my fellow bear guard sitting straight up in his bedroll, his wide eyes catching the light as he swung his flashlight in circles searching for the bear. Sure was nice to know he was keeping such a serious watch.

NOT MUCH OF A MULE

This is the story of Jasper who for most of his life at Rock Creek Pack Trains was "not much of a mule". Jasper was a medium sized, black john mule. When you needed to get him out of the corral, you could recognize him by a white mark just behind his ears. When I first knew him, he appeared to be just an average mule; middle-aged, average sized, medium build. He was sound and did an okay job of carrying his load. He didn't cause trouble in the station yard and seldom blew up while being loaded. The one thing he lacked that a really good pack mule needed on the rugged trails of the high Sierra was heart. All the packers knew that in any really tough situation where everything depended on a mule's courage, Jasper would most likely give up.

The first time I got to see Jasper in action was on an early season crossing of Mono Pass. Being the trip cook, I was leading a group of dudes on horseback. The pack strings had left the station about an hour behind us and were just catching us at the top of the pass. At almost 12,000 feet, parts of the trail were still covered with snow banks two or three feet deep. Previous trips had worn a trail through the snow. If you stayed on the packed trail, you were likely to be all right. I led my guests across a bank about 40 feet wide. Everyone did fine. Then we pulled off the trail so the strings could pass us after they crossed the snow. It was spectacular watching the matched black strings cross the sparkling snow high on the barren tundra of the pass. Then one of the middle mules stepped off the trail and bogged down in the snow. He thrashed around a little and then quit. Since a mule in trouble can pull your whole string down, the packer quickly untied ropes to free the rest of the string from the bogged mule. The other packer tied his horse and string and came down to help. Usually a bogged down mule will try to buck-jump his way out. He'll keep trying until he gets out, falls down, or until he's exhausted. This mule was only in about two and a half feet of snow, but he didn't even try to get out. The packers moved the other mules off the snow and came back for him with a horse. Hoping the extra pull would help him to move, they dallied up his lead rope and tried to lead him out. The mule just stood there like his feet were cemented to the mountainside. The boys unpacked him, but he still wouldn't try. Finally, they got the shovel off another mule's load and spent a fair amount of time digging all the snow out from under the mule. They also dug a short trail back to the place the rest of us had crossed. The mule decided that this would be good enough and finally strolled nonchalantly out of the snow. The tired packers had to drag the mule's load across the snow before they could put it back on him. As the packers finally passed us, I asked them what the heck was wrong with that mule. One of them said, "Oh, that's just Jasper. He's not much of a mule."

In an outfit with over a hundred head of stock, you might work with different animals on each trip. So it was several years before I found myself working around Jasper again. Not that I was all that disappointed to not have him around. On this trip we were northbound from Rock Creek to Mammoth. Since the guests on this trip were hikers, I rode with the packers and led a few mules, fortunately not Jasper. Head packer on this trip was the boss, Craig London, and in his string was our old friend Jasper. There is a beautiful spot on the John Muir Trail just below Pocket Meadow where the canyon is covered in wildflowers: lupine, fireweed, phlox, and pentstemon. Working your way through the jumbled flower-covered talus means your animals scramble from rock to rock up the many short switchbacks. Of course, it really gets bad if one of them decides to try to eat some of that tasty looking lupine at the same time they're jumping, sliding and scrambling up some big boulders. The worst spot was a switchback carved into the rock face. To make it more interesting, a large round boulder had rolled down and lay against the rock wall at the point of the turn. Of course, Jasper got in trouble, and of course it was right in that spot. Just as Jasper passed that corner, someone behind him stopped for a lupine snack and someone ahead of him tried to hurry his jump up the next set of rock steps. Stretched out between them Jasper lost his balance and sat down on the trail. Even with a pack load, most mules would have scrambled to their feet. But Jasper just sat there looking put upon. Craig undid the lead ropes so he was free of the other mules and yelled at him. Momentarily startled, Jasper started to heave himself to his feet. Half way up, he changed his mind and sat back down. Then he rolled slowly over backwards to land wedged between the round boulder and the rock face. With his pack load caught behind the boulder, he sat there like a fat man in a lawn chair. It was one of those moments when you have no real idea of what to do next, but for sure it wasn't going to involve any positive effort on Jasper's part. Craig didn't hesitate. He unfastened both pack cinches and the lash rope thereby freeing Jasper from his pack. Then he took the lead rope and standing straight in front of the mule put all his considerable strength into pulling 1100 pounds of mule uphill. To my complete surprise, he rolled that mule right forward and up on to his feet. Surprised Jasper as much as it did me. As before, the story ended with repacking Jasper. Craig never said anything against the mule, but I could tell he was thinking it.

For years Jasper went on working just hard enough not to get sold. And so eventually he reached his thirties still working for Rock Creek. At that age pack mules still work, but they do shorter moves and carry lighter loads on spot trips in close to the station. They don't work the long backcountry trips except for the Henkes trip. This is a 15 day hiking trip. The hikers are all a little long in the tooth, so the moves are short and the layover days are frequent. A perfect situation for the old-timer mules like Jasper. This particular trip was in the southern Sierra traveling the Pacific Crest Trail from Horseshoe Meadows to Shepherd Pass with a side trip down into the Kern Canyon. Near Mt. Whitney, this country is high and rough, but the trails are good, and the stock love the meadows. Jasper made it through 13 days without doing anything he shouldn't. The morning of the 14th day he was gone. Chris and Tom couldn't find him when they wrangled. It was a layover day, so they spent most of the day looking. Mules are herd animals and as a rule they don't go off by themselves. When you wrangle and come up short a single animal, it usually means the animal is sick, hurt, trapped, stolen, or dead. Craig joined the trip that day, coming in to help us get out over Shepherd Pass on the last day. He added his efforts to the search for Jasper, but there was no sign of him. Finally, out of time and out of places to look, sadly they gave up and moved out. Everyone agreed that Jasper had probably given up one last time and died out there somewhere.

It was late in the packing season and Rock Creek only had one more trip in the area where Jasper had disappeared. We hoped if he was still alive, he might join their stock. No such luck. Then about a week later, we heard a rumor about a wild black mule that had been seen at Junction Meadow. A few days after that there was another story about a stray mule that came by someone's camp at Crabtree. A few of us secretly hope it might be Jasper, but it wasn't all that likely. As the weeks of fall passed, hope faded. Winter in the high country can start as early as September, and any mule caught in heavy snow is done for. Then we heard that some people at Big Whitney Meadow had caught a loose mule, but it had broken free during the night. Big Whitney was off the main trail but was the way we had come on our trip. That's when we were sure it was Jasper. He was backtracking our trip and was only one more pass from the roadhead at Horseshoe Meadows. When he reached Horseshoe, packers from Cottonwood Pack Station tried to rope him but he got away. Finally, he got on the 12 miles of paved road that climbs down the east face of the Sierra from Horseshoe to Lone Pine. He marched right down that road ignoring traffic and anything else that might have gotten in his way. He was two miles from the outfit's winter pasture at Diaz Lake when a cattle guard and fences finally stopped him. By this time, he had been on the trail for close to three weeks covering almost 60 miles. He had refused to be stopped, caught or tied. Every stockman in the Eastern Sierra had been following the rumors and was rooting for Jasper to survive his great journey. So when Bob Olin from the Forest Service saw an old black mule standing in the middle of the road gazing toward Diaz pasture, he knew who it was. He caught him and called Craig. And that's how Jasper finally came home. And everybody working for the outfit had to admit that he was a lot more mule than any of us had ever thought.

BEARS ON CORA CREEK

Riding the breathtaking splendor of the High Sierra, smelling the sweet smell of Jeffery pines on the warm afternoon air, diving into the chilly waters of a high country lake, making life-long friends along the trail, enjoying coffee and music around the campfire…these are the moments that bring a person back to the high lonesome again and again. Warm and wonderful memories include almost everything in the Sierra, except perhaps, the bears. Smokey and Yogi aside, real bears are just not much fun. About the only thing they're good for is telling stories about them after whatever disaster they have precipitated is over. So, here is a bear story….

On a pack trip with Rock Creek we brought about a dozen riders and two strings of mules south out of Yosemite. The packers were Dave Dohnel and Richie Engle. Dave was tall, broad shouldered, with black hair and blue eyes. With looks right out of a romance novel, he was one of the partners in the outfit. Richie was a skinny kid just starting out in the packing business, but fated to make a fine hand. My name is Irene and I was the pack cook and dude wrangler for this illustrious group. Coming south over Isberg Pass was pretty rough going. I sorta thought that this pass might need the serious attention of a trail crew real soon, but with some care and a lot of luck we made it through without any real problems.

Our camp that night was a real pretty spot along Cora Creek. After such a long, hard day, we were really glad to get there. Without too much care we set up camp, turned the stock out, ate dinner and piled into our sleeping bags. Since we didn't know we were right in the middle of prime bear country, we slept long and peaceful. Since the bears didn't know we were there yet, they let us.

First thing the next day Richie went out on foot to wrangle the stock. Most of our packers liked to keep up a wrangle horse over night so they'll have one to ride in the morning, but Richie enjoyed going on foot like some of the old time packers did. He found the stock not too many miles from camp. Figuring on an easy day, he caught and bridled one of the riding horses and swung aboard. Gathering the animals, he headed them toward camp. Watching the stock in front swing around a grove of trees and out of sight, Richie concentrated on pushing the drags. Suddenly, the lead animals came stampeding back out of the trees. Horses and mules flew past Richie headed back the way they had come. Hanging on to his horse's mane, Richie spun around in pursuit of the herd. When he caught up with them, he circled them and started back. This time when he pushed them into the trees, they didn't run but they did refuse to go on. They snorted, shied and each one tried to work his way to the back of the herd.

Richie rode around the stalled herd to get a clear look at what kind of booger was up ahead. He figured it might be a bear. Well, it was three bears, all big and all between him and where he wanted to go. He scouted out a way around them and worked the herd down past them toward camp. Pretty clever for a new packer. The only problem was that the bears followed him. He made several tries at running them off, but that's a little difficult when the horse you're riding bareback really doesn't want to get anywhere near the bears. He actually did pretty well because by the time he reached camp only one bear was still with him. Of course, one bear is plenty if things work out the way they normally do.

So, a bear around camp in the daylight isn't usually too much trouble. They often go off and sleep until dusk. However, this bear found us more interesting than most. We caught glimpses of him off and on all day. In fact, when Dave was replacing the horse and mule shoes we'd lost over Isberg, I noticed that the bear was sitting about 60 feet away watching him shoe.

The guests spent the layover day resting up and hanging around camp. As it got toward evening Dave mentioned that the bear was still out there and that they should take care of their stuff. This means no food or anything that smells like food in the tents. All snacks and spare food needed to be turned in to the cook to be stored and guarded with the kitchen boxes. Additionally, many cosmetics attract bears and they should be treated like food or at least placed outside the tent. Left over lunch sacks also needed to be put in a safe place, not in the tent or left on the saddle. The guests on this particular trip were very experienced and had heard this talk a million times. Perhaps that was part of the problem.

Sitting around the campfire after dinner listening to their leader, Kathy, play the guitar, the guests all seemed relaxed and obviously were not worried about bears or much of anything else. Their tents were scattered loosely up the hill above the fire and the kitchen area. Not much in the way of snacks had been turned in for safekeeping so I thought it would be a good idea to remind them of Dave's warning. We talked about bears a little but they weren't too concerned. So I told a couple of scary bear stories. They were not impressed. Finally, I mentioned that they might want to move their tents in a little closer being as I could see the bear sitting between two of their tents enjoying the campfire show. They whipped around to stare and saw him sitting there among their tents, a big gray lump with eyes glowing in the firelight. That got their attention. Dave ran the bear off and the guests moved way faster than any other time that day. Within five minutes all the tents were in a tight circle way too close to the campfire and all the food was in the kitchen.

It was a long, long night. All the food was in wooden pack boxes. The boxes were covered with tarps. Pots and pans were scattered on top of the tarps to give warning if a bear tried to slide his head under the tarps for a taste. The cook, that's me, was sleeping next to the boxes. In a bad situation where you knew you had a persistent bear, you might tie a horse or mule in the camp, have a packer sleeping there or leave the lantern on. In this case we actually did all of these things. We tied a horse AND a mule in the kitchen, put a lighted lantern on the table, and had Dave sleep on the opposite side of the food boxes. Keep in mind that black bears weigh about 400 pounds, have impressive claws and teeth and are powerful enough to knock the front door off a cabin with one blow.

Fortunately they aren't as aggressive as grizzlies. That damned bear came into camp at least once an hour all night long. The stock would start stamping and snorting. Dave would jump up and yell, throw rocks, or beat on pans. I would do the same. Eventually, the bear would leave and we would try for a little sleep.

At 4:30 AM he came in for the last time. We chased him out again, then stood there exhausted and a little depressed discussing whether or not there was any point in trying for a little more sleep. Of course there wasn't. 4:30 is when you normally get up. While we were groaning and griping, Dave suddenly hissed, "Listen, what's that noise?" We stood and listened. It was a ringing bell-like noise. It came from the rocks above us and went "Ching ......ching ....ching." Dave was the first to figure it out. "It's a cinch ring hitting the rocks! The bear's got one of the saddles." He and Richie ran up into the rocks in time to catch the bear dragging off an expensive, custom-made saddle belonging to Kathy. They recovered it from the disappointed bear and returned it, scarred but intact. The owner shook her head in puzzlement as to why the bear would try to carry off her saddle. Perhaps the wet wipes with the nice fruit fragrance we found in the saddle bags could have had something to do with it.

A few hours later with the camp torn down and packed on the mules, we bid a fond farewell to "Bear Camp" on Cora Creek. As I looked back from the trail I saw the bear was still hanging around up in the trees and I thought he looked sad to see us go. Since he hadn't gotten any food from us I guess he was just missing the entertainment we had provided as we scrambled around camp all night trying to defend our supplies.

THE DUDE WHO WANTED TO SEE A BEAR

First off, we don't usually call our guests dudes, but sometimes you just can't think of a more likely term. Dudes isn't really an insult but it's usually used to point out someone who is a little more experienced at getting their coffee at Starbucks than off the camp cookfire. The dude in question was a lady and for the most part pretty nice. She and her husband joined us for a 12 day trip from Rock Creek to Tuolumne Meadows. Dave Dohnel, a mighty handsome packer and partner in the outfit, Matt Campbell, a big blond horseman from San Luis Obispo, and I were working this trip. My name's Irene and I was the grumpy old pack cook who was wrangling this group.

The itinerary for the first half of this trip took us from Mono Pass to Silver Pass and across the head of Cascade Valley. High lonesome passes, wildflower sprinkled meadows, tumbling waterfalls, and sparkling lakes enlivened this portion of the trail. After the pretty stuff, the move from Tully Hole to Deer Creek was long, dusty, and tedious. That night at Deer Creek wasn't memorable except for the fact that I made a fool of myself. I was pretty tuckered out so I went to bed while the packers were still talking around the campfire. The last thing I heard as I drifted off was the mention of some bear tracks one of them had seen as they were approaching camp.

In the middle of a pretty dark night something woke me up. There was just enough moonlight to see shapes and about six feet from my bedroll there was in fact a big, dark shape. It wasn't moving but you could see that it had a low heavy body, a big head and a definite snout. The weak moonlight was shining off its eye. Putting all available information together with lightning speed, I leaped to the conclusion that there was a bear in my kitchen. I leaped from my bed yelling, "Bear! Bear! There's a bear in the kitchen!" As the people around me began to stir, I was embarrassed to realize that the big shape was not a bear after all. It was just the coffee pot on the campstove. Ducking back down into my sleeping bag, I mumbled, "Never mind. It's okay. Go back to sleep." I was sure glad that it was too dark for anyone to see how red my face was.

The next morning as we got ready to move to Johnson Lake, I tried to ignore any mention of bears. That move was down right interesting. We traveled past volcanic cinder cones, dropped down an enormous canyon wall covered in dark, brooding red firs, picked up supplies at Reds Meadows, rode the John Muir Trail above Devils Post Pile, and finally above Minaret Falls came to Johnson Meadows. Along the trail we came upon some riders we knew from Owens Valley. We traveled together for a short while and during that time one of the guys in the other group had a helacious wreck. His horse threw a fit and bailed off the trail. The horse rolled all the way to the bottom of the hill with his rider under him. He survived, and Dave and I walked him back up to the trail, while his partner went in search of his horse. Luckily suffering no more than a mild concussion, we left him in the care of his riding partner and moved on. When his horse had bailed off the trail into midair, he narrowly missed taking several of us with him. With that in mind I noticed that several of our guests had pale faces and pretty big eyes as we rode on up to the lake.

Johnson is a lovely spot right by the Muir trail where Minaret Creek flows into a lake. There are big firs, aspens, a meadow, and several great swimming holes. Johnson is well known for the "singing tree". The tree is a burned out aspen that is still standing. It leans against another aspen and the burned holes make weird music whenever the wind blows. As always the late afternoon consisted of building camp, a quick swim to clean up, cooking dinner, and cleaning up the kitchen afterward. That night I left the remains of a chocolate pie out on the table for late snackers. Everything else was tarped and booby-trapped with pans. In my bedroll near the kitchen, I lay listening to the packers talking about football. For some reason that put me right to sleep. When I woke up later, it was quiet and, except for a few glowing coals in the campfire pit, dark. I lay there listening to the night and then I saw the "bear" shape from the night before. I laughed to myself knowing that I wouldn't let that old stove fool me a second time. Then the dark shape turned and breathed in my face. Did I ever mention that bears have really bad breath? They do and it was.

I lay still until the bear strolled on into the kitchen. Then I started yelling for the packers. The bear was by the table checking out the chocolate pie. Dave jumped up out of his bed and shined his light on the bear. Things were getting busy enough to make the bear uncomfortable. So he grabbed the pie tin in his mouth and took off down the trail. With only his flashlight, bare feet and wearing only his skivvies, Dave took off after the bear. As the yelling faded into the distance, I wondered a little about what Dave had in mind. About ten minutes later he walked back into camp. When I asked what happened, he said, "I chased that bear about a hundred yards. At that point, the bear stopped, turned to face me, and growled. It occurred to me that I might have chased him far enough, so I came back to camp." Right then, I was glad that the bear was gone and I think Dave was glad he hadn't caught him. The bear was probably glad he had the pie. The only dissatisfied person was the lady I mentioned earlier.

She was mad that we hadn't awakened her before we chased off the bear. She figured a bear was part of the entertainment and, by golly, she wanted to see it. I considered sending her down the trail to look for the bear, but decided that that sounded pretty snotty even for me.

After two more moves over Island Pass and Donohue Pass, we reached our last campsite in Yosemite. The Lyle Fork of the Tuolumne has lots of bears, so I figured that my lady dude might get her wish. Sitting around the campfire late into the evening, everyone was doing the kind of storytelling that happens at the end of a trip. Nobody much noticed when the dude lady left for a trip to the privy. The night was split by her screams as she tore back to the campfire. "Bear! There's a bear in the privy!" she screamed. All the big, strong men (packers and guests alike) headed for the privy to chase off the bear. Yelling didn't seem to impress the big old sow at all. Upping the ante they turned lights on her and pounded on pans. She moved off but circled right back. Finally, throwing sticks and rocks, they drove her down to the river and across it.

The men returned to the campfire, bragging loudly about their wilderness savvy. In a while the lady dude headed back up to the privy. Almost immediately she was running back to the fire again screaming that there was a bear in the privy. Taking the guys back to the privy, she pointed up. In the top of the trees was a pair of twin bear cubs. Everyone stood there real quiet as the realization of what they had done seeped into their brains. They had driven a bear sow away from her cubs and lived to tell about it. Without a word, they drifted silently back to the campfire. Aside from a little subdued conversation, everyone at the fire just sat and waited. About an hour later Dave checked the privy and the cubs were gone. I guess the sow had come back for her kids. Nobody said much, just sorta slipped quietly off to bed.

The next day, after a several hours of easy riding down the meadow along the river, we ended our trip in Tuolumne

Meadows. As we approached the trailhead and its campgrounds, I noticed lots of signs with information about bears, but for some reason our lady dude seemed to have lost interest in them. Guess she'd seen all the bears she wanted to see.

JUST RIDIN' AND WORRYIN'

In the old time cowboy movies they are always riding down the trail singing. This works in the mountains, too, unless you have the kind of voice that would scare the stock. Sometimes you spend all your time watching your animal's footing in the rocks. If you are leading a string of mules, you spend most of your ride looking back, checking on the string's progress. On an easy day you can take time to smell the pines and the trail dust, catch the sun's glint off a miniature waterfall in an avalanche chute, feel the morning sun on your back, or just watch the cloud shadows race over the cliffs and valleys. Your dudes are sure to be enjoying the sights of high lakes nestled under towering cliffs, wading through knee-high wild flowers, and watching wildlife. Mostly they're enjoying being free from the worries of home and office. Since they don't have to worry, you do. So, often, the long quiet rides provide you with a chance to catch up on your worrying. Let me tell you about one trip where we got to do a lot of worrying.

This was a nine day loop trip south from Mono Pass to Pine Creek. We had nine hikers for guests and a crew of three. Howard and Bryan were packing and I was cooking and worrying. A quick list of the worries we started out with would include: long, hard moves, older hikers including one that was 70, packers that had never been in this section of the Sierras before, the fact that we had no hiking guide, and an unfortunate newspaper article. That newspaper article painted me as some kind of mountain legend and unfortunately all these guests had seen the paper. Since I turned out to be just another little old lady (albeit one on mule back), they were pretty disappointed. My two packers did turn out to be genuine heroes on this trip, but since Howard is a big gruff guy and Bryan never talks, the guests didn't get a chance to realize what the boys had been through.

Traveling over the stark beauty of 12,000 foot Mono Pass and down the aspen graced length of Mono Creek Canyon made our first two moves pretty simple. The only real worries at that point had to do with the fact that I had discovered that the outfitter had left out one night's dinner. Well, so what if we were missing a meal. I would come up with something...... I hoped. The other problem had to do with getting where we were going. Without a hiking guide, I had to spend lots of time explaining each day's route to the hikers. Careful, detailed descriptions of every trail, water crossing, turn and campsite were necessary to avoid spending the night searching for lost hikers. "Wait for me at the crossing" were, temporarily anyway, the most important words in the English language.

The third day when we moved from Quail Meadows to Bear Creek was a truly great day for worrying. As we crossed the bridge over Mono Creek, I started to worry about the missing meal. Mainly we were missing a ham and everything to go with it. But I quit wondering what to do about it when I noticed that a partly fallen aspen tree was caught on the pack on Bryan's second mule. Holding my breath, I watched as the leaning aspen rode up and over the load and then settled back to rest in the fork of another tree. I only had time to think, "My God, what if that had fallen?" when the fourth mule's load caught the same tree. It was lifted out of the fork it was resting in and carried along until it slid off the load and fell toward the rump of the mule. At that moment the top of the falling tree caught in some branches that held it up until all the mules had passed safely under it. Howard and I looked at each other and each let out a big breath. Bryan just rode on down the trail. We never told him about the trees till much later. Now what had I been worrying about? Oh, yeah, what about the missing ham? Well, what if I stole some beef from some other dinners and made a stew instead?

This was where we reached the wooden causeway over a long boggy section of trail. The causeway was very handy but also very old. The last time I had crossed it one board was broken through and the animals had to step over the hole. Bryan was around a blind corner when he reached this spot. I figured that's where he was because there was lots of yelling and some crashing sounds up ahead. When I rounded the corner, it became obvious that the hole now involved two of the foot-wide boards. An animal would have to jump to cross it, and Bryan and his string had already done so. My mule, Abby, jumped it easily but I was thinking about Howard's string. He had several huge, powerful mules that would have a hard time jumping the hole. It was also possible that their weight would shatter another weakened board. They made it across, but it was awe inspiring to see 1500 pound mules like Glen and Bertha launch themselves and a couple of hundred pounds of pack over the break in the causeway. After another sigh of relief, we started up the never-ending switchbacks on Bear Ridge. It takes over two hours for a horse to climb to the top. For a while I worried about how our guests would do on the daunting climb. Then thoughts of the missing dinner crept into my head. I figured if I saved my own steak from the next dinner, kept any leftover steak, and cut about two and a half pounds of meat off of the eight pound roast I had, it would be enough to make stew. I had some extra carrots and could swipe an onion from the sandwich makins. If I saved any left over corn, I would be all set except for potatoes and dumplings.

As the Bear Ridge trail got higher and steeper, we came upon our next obstacle. The entire trail was blocked by a fallen tree. It was a huge red fir that was about six feet thick where it lay across the trail. The hillside was far too steep to take the animals off the trail to get around the tree. We would have to cut our way through. Now, Rock Creek axes are infamous for their lack of a sharp edge. Fortunately Howard had his own personal axe and began to hack away at the tree. With his thick arms, powerful shoulders, and red beard, Howard looked more like Paul Bunyan than a packer. Now I had a whole new set of things to worry about. What if Howard couldn't cut a hole big enough for the animals to squeeze through? The guests were ahead of us. What would they do if we couldn't get through with their food and bedrolls? What if Howard's ground level cuts caused the tree to slide farther down the hill? It could completely close the trail and maybe even crush Howard between the butt of the log and the shattered stump. Cutting through the tree was a brutal job, and Howard and Bryan took turns chopping. You know, in the hour and a half it took them to cut through that tree, I never once thought about cooking. Finally, he had a big enough hole to squeeze a mule through. Unstringing the mule we squeezed them one at a time through the narrow gap. Finally we were back on the move.

Headed on up the last third of the switchbacks, I remembered that I was supposed to be worrying about the possibility of hitting ground hornets. Ground hornets are just what the name sounds like; hornets that live in holes in the ground. When anything walks over their hole, they come boiling out and sting the daylights out of everything within about 50 feet of the hole. The only thing you can do is whip your animals up and get out of there in a hurry. If this happens where it is particularly steep or rugged, a stampede of terrified mules can lead to a helluva wreck. Nearing the top of the switchbacks, the ground began to level out. Just a few more turns and we would be on the pumice plateau that is the top of Bear Ridge. I turned around to congratulate Howard on getting us safely up the hill. Just then I noticed that his second mule, Glen, was inventing what appeared to be a new dance. He jumped in the air, danced sideways, kicked up his hind legs, and then repeated that in the opposite direction. My first impression was that he was teaching it to the other mules because they began doing the same thing. I hollered, "Run, Howard! You've got ground wasps!" With very little encouragement, his whole string stampeded up the hill. Bryan and I also ran like hell just to get out of their way. About 200 yards from the wasp nest we finally got all the stock stopped and quieted down. With only a few minor stings, everyone seemed to be okay.

The trip across the ridge and down to Bear Creek was relatively easy. There was one more down tree but it was much smaller, and someone had already bushwhacked a trail around it. A couple of loads worked loose on the steep downhill but were easily retied. I was too tired to do much superfluous worrying, so I confined my thoughts to worrying about when we would meet our guests along the trail and how I could be sure of getting them to camp. As it gets toward the end of the day exhaustion often leads hikers to make errors. As we passed the groups of guests along the trail, I reminded them to wait for me at the crossing so that I could lead them down the other side of the creek to camp. When we finally crossed the creek, we were only 200 yards from the camp. Since none of the hikers were there yet, I decided to show the packers where the camp was so that they could start unpacking while I went back for the guests. Sounded logical at the time.

A hundred feet out of camp we crossed our last obstacle; a rocky, dry creek bed. Bertha, 1500 pounds of round red mule, didn't like the looks of the creek bed and pulled back. After several tries, the big mules ahead of her dragged her across. She took it in one huge leap. That was one leap too many for the leather strap holding one of the aluminum food boxes to her saddle. The metal bracket cut through the leather strap and 80 pounds of food swung down the mule's side. As her pack load came apart, it began shedding top loads all around her. She panicked and tried to run away, but tied head and tail to the other mules, she tangled all of them into one big wreck. Thrown off balance by the disintegrating pack load, with her feet tangled in the ropes, she crashed to the ground and rolled onto her back wedged into a grove of young pine trees. Unable to move, she lay gasping as the lead rope from the mule behind her slowly strangled her. Handing me his string, Bryan joined Howard in cutting the ropes that held Bertha to the other mules. Now she could breathe, but couldn't get up. This is where experience counts and these boys had it. They removed the pack boxes and spilled food. Then they unfastened her pack saddle and rigging, pulling her cinches out from under her. With no weight on her she could get up if she could get her feet under her. But this time her feet were straight up in the air. The boys looped ropes over her pasterns and bracing themselves, rolled her over onto her side. She sat up, looked around, and got up. She was shaking, sweating and a little scraped up, but basically okay. Amazingly, so was most of the food. The one thing that gave us a laugh was that a large glass jar of pickles had fallen out of the box onto a flat rock, rolled around in a circle, spun like a coin on a table, and stopped up right and unbroken with its label facing us like it was on display in the grocery store.

Howard and Bryan checked Bertha over, gave her a few pats and then went back to work. They put up a picket line, tied the animals and started unloading supplies in camp. I rode back up to the crossing to make sure the guests all could find the camp. Being as we had left 13 sets of tracks and put on a major mule fiasco in plain site of the trail, I really didn't worry about missing any guests. I guess that I had forgotten that my real job was to worry. I probably should have because when I got to the trail one of the guests was yelling at me for not being at the crossing when she got there. She screamed that she couldn't find her mother and that my dereliction had probably allowed her mother to wander off up the trail to be lost in the wilderness. I rode up the trail far enough to be sure that her mother hadn't gone that way then I returned. She yelled at me some more when I tried to tell her that her mother was most likely in camp waiting for us. I tried to explain that we had had an emergency with the mules and I had had no choice. She said that she had watched us "fooling around" with that mule but couldn't find the camp. Since the wreck was actually at the camp, I sorta ran out of things to say and just rode back down to the camp. Her mother was there and was fine. I bit my tongue and resisted telling the daughter that if she hadn't hiked off and left her mother alone on the trail, every day of the trip, she might not have had to worry about her so much.

The following day was a layover day, and boy did we need the rest. The boys repaired Bertha's broken pack equipment, shod mules and horses that had lost shoes on the trail, and went swimming in the creek. I cooked and washed dishes, cleaned my pack boxes, did some laundry and, of course, worried. Now this kind of worrying is most like a dog "worrying" a bone. My mind just keeps chewing at a problem until it gets a solution. I was still working on the missing dinner. It was going to be stew, but I still needed potatoes and dumplings. They had sent huge potatoes for me to bake with the steak dinner. So I would cut them in half, wrap them in foil, and bake them in the coals. I would save the rest for the stew. That would be a little cheesy, but most women on these trips only take half a baked potato anyway. And all of our guests, but one, were women. Okay, so what about the dumplings?

I had a box of biscuit mix, but it was supposed to be the crust for a peach cobbler for tonight's dinner. This is where the problems start to multiply. To use the biscuits for the stew, I had to find another way to make dessert for tonight. Well, I had canned peaches and whipped cream to work with. Being on a layover, I also had the luxury of being able to actually look through my supplies instead of just working from memory. The turning point was when I found a package of pecan shortbread cookies. I crushed them up, added butter and baked them into a crust in the bottom of a flat pan. I made a heavy sugar syrup and reduced it to a glaze. I arranged the peaches on the shortbread crust, topped them with the glaze and served it with the whipped cream. It looked real pretty and tasted okay. I was almost as proud as when we got Bertha out of the trees alive. The rest of the trip went pretty well and we only had to think our way out of a few more problems. I started tying my big blue scarf to a tree whenever we had a turn off that the hikers might not be sure of. Howard did a little clever thinking, too. One morning he needed to wake me up, and I was really out. He yelled and threw things, but I just slept on. So he went into the kitchen and opened a pack box. Conditioned by years of guarding the food from bears, I was on my feet in under a second. Pretty smart guy. Oh, yeah, we had stew for dinner the last night and it was pretty good.

THE GRAY BAND AT MCBRIDE

When you work for Rock Creek in the Eastern Sierra, not all your trips are with pack strings through the high lonesome of the Sierra crest. You might ride fence on the 6,000 acre winter graze in Owens Valley, or take dudes on the horse drive, or you might go to the Pizona to watch wild horses which is the most fun of all.

The mustang trips are a series of four day trips in the pinyon country along the Nevada border east of Mono Lake. These trips take place in May and June before the snow has melted off the high passes in the mountains. The outfit sets up a base camp with tents, showers, corrals, and a permanent kitchen with a real live chef. The supplies come in by 4-wheel drive. The guests and guides come in on horseback. Best of all, old pack cooks get to just ride, guide, track, and watch wild horses all day, every day.

When you first meet your dudes, you get to teach them about wild horse bands and about the hand signals you will use to communicate without spooking out the mustangs. You will show them the mustang trails and the stud piles, the difference between the tracks of animals that are grazing and those that are on the move. You will show them the tracks of predators such as bears, coyotes, and mountain lions. You will also teach them practical stuff like "never squat in a bush with a rattlesnake in it".

You will discuss horse behaviors and give them the info from the books where it talks about bands of mustangs. Most harem bands are from five to a dozen horses and are made up of one stallion, his mares and their foals. Bachelor bands are groups of two to five young stallions who have banded together after being run off their mothers' bands as yearlings. They stay together until they are strong enough to fight for their own harem band. Old stallions who have lost their bands to stronger studs often just wander around alone. But in real life it seems that horses often stray from these neat categories.

The first time I saw a band with more than one stallion was the gray band at McBride. This was a band of five horses; one black, one bay, one dun, and two grays. The first time I saw this particular band, they were out in the middle of a high sage flat called McBride. We tied our own horses out of sight and crept up to a basaltic ridge to watch them. Mustangs will spook out if they see you as a threat, so watching them requires a lot of tricks; don't talk, stay down, take off your hat, use binoculars, and don't wear white. Once you get where you can see them, watch what they're doing and figure out what that tells you.

This band was grazing out in the open where nothing could sneak up on them. The first obvious thing about them was that the two grays were mares, since they were heavy in foal. So this was a harem band rather than a bachelor band. When a harem band moves, the horse in front picking the route is the boss mare and the one herding from the back and defending them is the stallion. The stallion also stays between the mares and any possible threat. Using these criteria, we decided that the black was the stud and the bay was probably the boss mare. But what about the dun?

The dun stayed about forty feet away from the group of other horses. It was moving around, grazing, but it never moved toward the other horses. After a while we got a good enough look to realize that the dun was another stallion. Someone suggested that he might be a yearling that hadn't been run out of the herd yet. Closer looks showed that he was too old for that; both too large for a yearling and having a mane that was over two feet long. A mane like that means a horse is at least three years old, probably older. So what the heck was he doing?

The first things to become obvious were that the black stud was not comfortable with the dun stud that close, and that he kept moving so that he was always between the dun stud and the mares. The black horse seemed to be watching for one wrong move. The dun horse kept his head down grazing and was very careful not to look at the mares. His body behavior seemed to say, "See I'm just out here grazing. I'm not interested in your mares." As we watched we guessed that he was an older stud who had lost his mares to a stronger challenger and wanted to hang out with this band. Or maybe he meant to get the band for himself?

At one point during the time we were watching, a lone rider on horseback cut across the flat. It was Tom, one of our packers, and he knew enough to angle away from the horses to keep from spooking them. As he passed by at about 100 yards, the black horse and his boss mare shifted the herd so the mares were protected by the stud. The really interesting part was that he kept moving them until the dun horse was left out there between the band and the lone rider. It's hard to tell whether he was using the dun as a buffer or just trying to get both of his enemies where he could watch them at the same time. The dun kept right on grazing and pretending that he wasn't interested in the herd.

After the rider had passed, the dun horse decided that he needed to roll in a nearby dust wallow. To get there in a straight line, he had to walk within ten feet of the mares. As he did this he kept his eyes straight ahead and never looked at the mares, but his head and tail carriage seemed like he was feeling pretty snorty. The black stud became more and more agitated. He threw up his head, pawed the ground, and wove from foot to foot. He couldn't seem to decide if he was being challenged or not.

When the dun reached the wallow, he pawed the dust and took a nice long roll. At this point, the black finally decided that he was being challenged. Or maybe he just realized that the dun was at a disadvantage in the wallow. Anyway, the black let out a scream and charged after the dun. The dun jumped to his feet, and they crashed into each other chest to chest. The dun was slammed to the ground but quickly scrambled to his feet and ran for his life. After a while, he circled wide around the band and returned to his grazing spot, again pretending to ignore the mares. The black returned to his guard station between the mares and the dun, waiting for the next move in this equine soap opera.

During the several hours when we were watching these horses, another rider slipped up behind us. It was Wes with a message from the boss. It seemed that he and his group were watching us from a ridge above the flat and wanted a better view of the grey band. So would we leave and let them come down to our spot. I wouldn't have minded sharing, but this message seemed a bit unfair. So I sent Wes back with a simple message. It was, "No." It occurred to me later that I was almost as protective of my people as that old black stud was of his band.

Now, it was getting late and we had several hours of riding to reach camp before dinner. So we slipped quietly away leaving the grey band still grazing on the flats at McBride.

I SEE BY YOUR OUTFIT THAT YOU ARE A COWBOY

Return with me once again to the packing days in the High Sierra. As you may remember from past tales, I am Irene, the little round pack cook, guide and occasional storyteller. I travel the high lonesome with many of the great and not-so-great in the horse packing business. Over the years I have seen many kids come to the mountains as useless, young gunsels. It's surprising how many of them turn into genuine hands in only a year or two. Of course we also get the occasional "Hollywood cowboy" who arrives with a lot of talk and not much else. Most of them don't last a season, but some stay on for a while. They usually leave just about as green as they came except now their stories are longer. The only real advantage to having one of these guys around is that the single female guests are sometimes harboring a "western romance novel" fantasy about an affair with a "real cowboy" and these guys are willing to be part of that fantasy. Most of these guys were pretty good looking which I'm sure was part of the problem. These kinds of guys don't do much work but they do keep the guests happy. Since I don't have much patience with them, they're usually not too fond of me either.

WARNING: The following tales contain considerable badmouthing. If you are offended by negative opinions, please go to another story.

Well, first off there was Ted. We worked together at Mt. Whitney Pack Trains when he first came to Owens Valley. In later years he worked for some of the local ranches, so maybe he finally earned his spurs. At the time I knew him, he was pretty green but tried real hard to convince everyone that he knew more about stock than any other living person. That made him pretty hostile to anyone who questioned his abilities. I remember one time when he was loading up the final string for a Trail Riders trip leaving out of Horseshoe Meadows. All the other strings had already pulled out and I was waiting to bring up the drag. What was slowing Ted down was that he kept wasting time talking about how good he was. Finally he started bragging that he could tie a diamond hitch faster than anybody, maybe under 30 seconds. Being tired of his mouth and having little ability to control my own, I drawled that I had in fact tied a diamond in twelve seconds flat. Now that wasn't exactly a lie. I just didn't mention that at the time I was practicing on a set of empty boxes thrown over the hitching rail. Taking up the challenge, Ted said that if a useless little bitch like me could tie in twelve seconds, by God, he could tie in ten. In his enthusiasm, he put a little extra swing on his lash cinch and instead of whipping it over the top of the pack load and under the mule, he threw it about 20 feet up a pine tree. When several hard pulls failed to dislodge it, he was forced to climb the tree to get his cinch back. Since the tree was a young lodgepole with lots of close packed, bristly branches Ted had quite a battle to retrieve his rope. By the time he emerged looking like he'd lost a fight with a bobcat, I was laughing pretty hard. That night the boss bawled me out for causing Ted to waste more time. He was right and I was ashamed, but darn, it was funny.

Another memorable moment from my years with Ted came at Crabtree Meadows. Since we had a really long move over the top of Whitney the next day, the stock had been turned loose for the day and would be tied up that night. The stock had drifted west for several miles and were over to Big Sandy. It was Ted's job to wrangle the stock and bring them in. For whatever reason, he chose a big, white gelding to wrangle on. Try to picture this. Everyone is sitting in camp having dinner. The sunset is painting the western sky in blazing colors. Ted on his big, white horse rides directly into that sunset as everyone watches. Reaching the other side of the meadow, he stops abruptly causing his horse to rear. Forty people, all struck by the same thought, yell, "Hi! Ho! Silver." The only thing that sorta wrecked it was that Ted rode all the way back to ask what the shouting was about. We were laughing too hard to tell him.

The only time Ted and I really got into it was on another trip to Crabtree. It was one of those trips where everyone ate like a horse. This can be a real problem for the cook. She has to save out food to make sure the packers are well fed. If they aren't getting enough to eat, they can't do the kind of hard work that makes up their jobs. You have to feed the guests enough to keep them happy and yet limit them to keep the packers going. The cook eats last and if there isn't enough that's just too bad. It's part of the job. Of course, if you're built like me, you can last several weeks on fat alone. On our last night at Crabtree everyone got good sized firsts but there were no seconds. The only thing left was two biscuits. As I hadn't had anything to eat since dinner the night before this, I figured those biscuits were mine. Being as they were my whole dinner I planned to savor them after I finished the dishes. I set them on the kitchen box thinking about the possibility of hunting up some jam to go with them. While I was drying the dishes, Ted came into the kitchen. He spotted those biscuits and said that since he particularly liked biscuits, he was going to take them. I told him not to as they were my dinner. He made a rude sound and grabbed for them anyway. Since I had a spatula in my hand, I smacked his fingers with it. He turned to leave and I put the spatula down. As he stepped away, he called me some pretty creative names. Somewhat offended, I planted the sharp toe of my riding boot where it would do the most good. Ted swung around with one fist clenched and came after me. Reaching behind me for the spatula, I accidentally came up with a butcher knife instead. When I held it in front of me, Ted changed his mind about hitting me. He left the kitchen without further comment. Years later at Reds Meadow I heard a packer tell this story only in that version I had knifed a packer for being in my kitchen. At least I didn't have any trouble keeping people out of my kitchen while I worked at that outfit.

While I was working at Reds Meadows, I ran into another one of these gold-plated cowboys. This one was named Bill and he was actually a pretty experienced hand with horses and mules. It was dealing with people that brought out the phony in him. He was one of those fellows who never, ever take off their cowboy hats because they don't want anyone to know that they are bald. The first trip I took with him was a four day trip to Thousand Island Lake. We had two layover days and his job was to care for the stock and take the guests on day rides. Early on the first layover he didn't eat breakfast and when I went to see how he was doing with the stock, he was lying on his bedroll groaning and retching. Since he was too sick to work I did all his work as well as my own. It wasn't until late the third day that I caught him laying on his bedroll eating a sack of cookies he had swiped from the kitchen. He hadn't been sick at all. I guess he was pretty proud of what a fool he had made of the new cook.

A few years later I ran into Bill again. I was working with a great little gal named Kathy. She drove 18 wheelers in the winter and was a pack cook in the summer. She was young and cute and pretty much liked all the packers. Old Bill and she had a brief go around which Bill took way too seriously. He decided he was in love with her and started stalking her. One day between trips a bunch of us were sitting out by the big stump back of the store when Bill came out of his cabin. He called Kathy over to him and said that he was in love with her and if she didn't love him in return he would kill himself. She said that since she didn't love him that might be a problem. He turned and went back in the cabin, slamming the door. A few minutes later we were all startled by the sound of a gunshot. The cabin door swung open and Bill staggered out, a gun in his hand. He slumped to the ground, the gun falling in the dirt near his outstretched fingers. As I sat there too stunned to react, I noticed that the other crew members were gradually getting to their feet and drifting silently away. One girl walked to Bill and I thought she was going to help him. But she just stepped over him, and went on to her cabin. Kathy was still sitting next to me and said, "Don't worry. He does this all the time." Then she left, too. After a few minutes, Bill raised his head and looked around. Seeing that his audience had left, he got up and dusted himself off. Picking up his gun, he went back to his cabin. Guess this kind of stuff keeps the job from being boring.

At Rock Creek I ran into Grippo, another member of the brotherhood of gunsels. He was a saddle maker who came every summer and traded a week of fixing pack equipment for a week of playing like he was a real live packer. After a few years of that he was so convinced that he was a packer that he managed to convince the administration of a community college that he was, too. They hired him to teach a packing class. The first summer I met him he brought a group of his adult students on a learning trip. Might have been kinda fun if he'd known what he was doing.

He started out by informing me that I didn't have to worry if this trip was too much for me because he had another cook along with him if I couldn't handle it. Since I had twenty-five years of experience cooking for groups ranging from three people to a hundred people, I was somewhat offended by his greeting. I was hoping that his packing skills were better than his people skills, but I was soon disappointed. On the first day the regular packers took their strings and went on ahead. Grippo showed his people how to pack one mule and then brought it with us. One mile up the trail the load fell off. I could see it was going to be a long day and an even longer trip. After repacking the mule, Grippo left that mule in the care of one of his guests. He then dropped to the back of the string to ride drag. We got over the top of the pass without further mishap. Later as we rode along the side of Summit Lake, I heard a horse coming up along the line of riders at a dead run. Since we were just under 12,000 feet in elevation, I knew that no one in their right mind would be willingly running a horse. Expecting a panicked guest on a run away, I pulled my little mare, Goose, out of line to try and block the fast closing animal. It was Grippo, smiling a big shit-eating grin while galloping his horse to the front. I was pissed enough to yell some pretty interesting advice to him which I can't repeat here. Then I made him walk his heaving horse back to the end of the line. He's lucky I didn't make him walk to camp.

You know, if I tell you all the stupid things he did on that one trip, this story will be a book. But if I was going to, I would mention when he set off the firecrackers and spooked all the stock out of camp. Realizing that everyone was pissed about it, he tried to blame it on some backpackers and offered to lead a group of guys over to beat up the innocent campers. Another clever move was the day he made everyone unsaddle without tying up because the horses might catch their saddles in the picket rope. That left the saddles scattered all over camp which cost an hour to clean up. The next morning he had everyone tie their horses on the picket line before saddling, then left the horses standing tied for the next hour. Near as I can figure, he musta thought that horses only tangle their saddles in the picket line in the afternoon, but not in the morning.

The worst thing he did was one afternoon when I had snacks out before dinner. The old Rita mule was trying to sneak in to snatch some crackers. I woulda chased her off, but Grippo started feeding her stuff off the table, petting her, and telling his followers about what a great mule she was. When they turned their backs to go to the campfire, he muttered "Goddamn pet mule" and slugged Rita as hard as he could right in the nose. Didn't seem very fair to me.

During this trip Grippo rode with all the packer hopefuls. I took care of the people who were just there for the ride. This included one lady who had never ridden before and was six months pregnant. She got the riding down pretty well but still had trouble mounting. I just made do by having her use any available rock or log for a mounting block. One day her horse developed a cinch sore. We stopped on the trail and I rigged her cinch so it didn't touch the sore. It wasn't ideal because I couldn't rerig both sides of the saddle as the right side was missing the back cinch ring. Just as I was helping her get up on a log to mount, Grippo and his group caught up with us. Unfortunately he decided to get involved. First he started yelling at the lady guest for using the log. Then he tried to force her to mount from the ground. Her pregnancy made that very difficult and she couldn't get on. Then he noticed the changed rigging on the saddle and demanded to know why it was like that. I showed him the cinch sore. Then he noticed that the rigging was different on the off side. So he took the whole saddle off the horse, all the while lecturing me on how having it rigged two different ways could torque the saddle and sore the horse's back. Instead of defending my decision, I tried to tell him that it was the only thing you could do since the back ring was missing on the off side. He went right on working on the saddle and telling me about all my basic flaws. Then he gathered all his students in close so he could show them how it should have been done. When he went to put the offside billets through the back ring, he discovered there wasn't one. At this point he started cussing and just went right on cussing while he put the saddle back together exactly as it was when he got there. Still cussing he saddled the horse, mounted his own horse, took his guests and rode off. That left me to take my guest and her horse back to the log where we had been before we were so rudely interrupted. We only had two more miles to go that day and could change saddles that night, so the horse came out fine.

As the trip went on Grippo would give his students great, long lectures on how real packers did things. Most of the time he was wrong which wouldn't have been a problem for me if he hadn't been doing most of his speechifying in my kitchen while I was trying to work. Finally it reached the point where I was choking trying not to laugh at some of the stuff he was telling those folks. He took offense at my strangled hilarity and assured me that he would get me fired as soon as we got back to the station. Well, he tried, but I was lucky enough to have a good boss who listened to my side of the story, too. I was sure glad of that as it would have been really mortifying to get fired on the word of a gunsel.

TRAIL TO TEHIPITI

Not too long ago I was telling some stories about wrecks along the trail and I expressed the hope that talking about them wouldn't jinx me. Guess that was a futile hope. Most of the stories I tell were a long time back when I was young and foolish. This tale is about a trip just last summer when I was in my 60's and a long way from young but still pretty foolish. This trip should have been great, but between stock problems and dangerous trails, we had every kind of wrecks there were except maybe tyrannosaurus. Over the last twenty years at Rock Creek Pack Station, I have often heard the boss, Craig London, talk about sending a trip in toward Tehipiti Dome. Each time I would kinda perk up my ears, as all us packer folk love to go into new country. But in the packing business you go where the boss sends you and I never drew one of those trips.

The trips were always planned to go in over Bishop Pass, pick up the John Muir Trail southbound through LeConte Canyon, then turn west along the headwaters of the middle fork of the Kings River to Simpson Meadow. After a layover at Simpson you would take a three day side trip further down the Kings to Tehipiti Dome, the largest granite dome in the Sierra, and then back up to Simpson. From Simpson, you would climb the "bitch"

trail to Granite Pass and then out to Cedar Grove, a roadhead on
the west side. None of the previous trips actually completed the
whole itinerary. The way was blocked by landslides, forest fires,
or lack of maintenance. The nearest anyone came was fifteen
years ago when Mike Bottiani took a trip that did all of it except
the side trip to Tehipiti which was blocked by a landslide. We
weren't that lucky; we did the whole thing.

This summer, Craig announced that he had a group of
eight hikers who wanted to do the Tehipiti Trip. They were
the remnants of the old Henkes group, several other intrepid
hikers, and a former park ranger to serve as hiking guide. Joel,
a tall strong Texas boy, was our packer. I had worked with him
before, but on this trip my respect for him grew immensely as
I watched his strength, horsemanship, and common sense save
our bacon time and time again. Lisa, a sweet blonde Aussie gal
was Joel's wife and our second packer. My job was as pack cook
and occasional stock handler. Wes, a busted-up old hand like
me was along, but his exact job description was a little unclear.
Wes is a pretty fair packer and a great hand with the stock, but
early this summer he had gotten pretty badly trampled and was
still healing up from some broken ribs and bruised innards. After
seven weeks of enforced inactivity, Wes was bored enough that
he was pretty much making a pain in the butt of himself back at
the station. When he started getting the station cook too drunk
to work, Craig decided he better get him back on the trail. So he
added him to the Tehipiti trip. It was a little tricky because Craig
told us to be sure not to work Wes too hard, but Wes wanted to
feel that he was pulling his share of the load.

On this trip we would start out from Rainbow Pack Outfit
near South Lake out of Bishop. For a party this size you would
usually have the crew's four riding animals, eight to ten pack
mules, and a 'hospital' horse. The hospital horse is a riding
animal that is there for emergencies where a hiker is too hurt
to walk, but not in bad enough shape to need to be emergency

airlifted out of the backcountry. This includes things like blisters, sprains, or minor illnesses. When the animal isn't being ridden it serves as an extra pack animal, usually carrying grain loads. Normally, we would have had a couple of extra pack mules since an eleven day trip with no resupply would be going in real heavy on the food loads. Well, for our mules we had Pete, Floyd, Cootie, Rio, Aya, Em, Beau and Tony. As you can see, even having Red as the hospital horse left us with only nine head, which is a little short in the pack animal department. So the last day before the trip Craig decided to give us a spare mule. That would have been great except he gave us Queen. She is a tall red molly who was a great mule in her day. Unfortunately, her day was about thirty years ago.

As we packed up at Rainbow the first day, Craig was helping us get out. He put a fair sized duffel load on old Queen and tied her into Lisa's string. Everybody was packed pretty heavy and we faced a long climb in over Bishop Pass and down to Dusy Basin. I was riding drag and watching Queen real careful. She was carrying her load and dragging a reluctant Aya along behind her. I was really impressed that she was doing so well. I didn't realize that she was running purely on guts alone.

The Bishop Pass trail is a real pretty ride. It comes up out of South Lake through the aspens, willows and pines. It works its way up past a number of small alpine lakes and meadows until you reach the base of a set of broken red shale cliffs. This part of the trail is pretty steep and rocky. Reaching the top of the cliffs you traverse a huge flat snow bank and start down the other side toward Dusy Basin. We had no real problems except for the young mule dragging on Queen. Half way up we decided to give Queen a break. Joel moved her out of Lisa's string and onto the end of his own string where she wouldn't have to pull anyone along behind her. She did fine over the pass and down to camp. Then fifty yards from camp she tripped on a rock in the creek and went down. It took the whole crew, but mostly Joel, to get her unpacked and rolled up out of the creek and onto the grass. Even in a good position, she was too exhausted to get up. Finally, we left her there to recover while we unpacked and set up camp.

Dusy Basin is above 10,000 feet in the Kings Canyon National Park. That means no grazing and no campfires. Knowing I would have to cook on the Coleman stoves, I had planned an easy meal of stew, dumplings, salad and cake. While I put that together, Lisa and Wes finished unsaddling, hauled water, watered and picketed the stock, and dug a privy. Queen eventually felt good enough to get up and join the rest of the stock. Meanwhile Joel took three mules and rode a couple of miles back up the trail to haul the night's hay cubes to camp. Those cubes had been hauled most of the way in by a packer from Rainbow earlier that day.

After dinner I had to wash the dishes real fast because the temperature was down around freezing and my wash water was rapidly going from warm to cold to solid around the edges. The saddest thing about these high camps is that just where it is cold enough to really need a campfire, you can't have one. It was kinda pitiful to realize that the guests were all sitting in a circle around a bare space where the fire would have been in any other camp. Just then Rosie, a guest who was usually a real quiet loner, came up to me and asked, "What do you think of this?" She was holding what looked like a tuna can stuffed with cardboard. I asked her what it was and she said it was a campfire. She said she had made it at home by filling a tuna can with tightly rolled cardboard, pouring it full of paraffin, and adding a wick. It didn't look too promising, but what the heck. Maybe it would be better that nothing. At first we had trouble lighting the wick, but after a while the whole thing lit off. Rosie set it in the middle of the circle of cold tired people. It was nice and bright and made enough heat that you could warm your hands by it. Rosie's "campfire" sure made a difference in how everyone felt that night and to everyone's surprise lasted almost two hours.

The next day we moved from Dusy Basin to Grouse Meadow. It was all down hill as the trail dropped several thousand feet into LeConte Canyon. Except for one time when Joel's mare went down in the rocks below the big waterfall and later when we had some trouble finding a suitable camp, the day passed without incident. We packed Queen pretty light and I led her by herself. She did reasonably well and made it to camp without giving out.

At camp, Alden, our hiking guide and former ranger, made contact with a park service trail crew that was working down canyon from us. It seemed they had been working on the section of trail we were headed for. They still had a section of brush to clear but figured to have it done before we finished packing up in the morning. At first I was kinda flattered that the park was clearing trail just for us. Then I wondered what sort of country we were getting into if it was so little used that they hadn't had to clear the trail in a number of years. Putting that together with some talk I had heard at Rainbow the day we left, I started to have my doubts. You see, the boss at Rainbow had been reminiscing about using that canyon trail between LeConte and Simpson Meadow back in the old days. It seemed there were long sections where you needed to loose herd, and there was a section where a wrong step off the trail would drop you 80 feet into a thundering piece of river trapped in a slot of slick rock. Best of all there was a place called Devil's Washbowl where the drop into the river would put your animals into a whirlpool where they would be sucked down never to be seen again. Damn, I could hardly wait. However, Wes had been most of this way before and didn't seem all that worried. I sure hoped he was right.

So the next morning we headed out for Simpson Meadow. Just down canyon from our camp we passed the trail crew camp. No one was there, as they had been working down canyon since first light. The camp was empty except for a big doe that was eating someone's laundry off the line next to a tent. Before long

I could see that old Queen was going to be a problem. Every day we had made her load lighter so that now it was about 75 pounds. Still, she started dragging right away and if I pulled her she would stumble in the rocks. That was while we were still on the easy section of the trail before we turned off the Muir. At the turn off, I cut her loose and put her in front of me. The rest of the strings seemed to be doing fine.

The ten miles of trail from the Muir turnoff to Simpson Meadow were a real revelation. There was very little canyon bottom, just steep canyon walls, cliffs and a big old roaring river down below. The trail itself showed signs of recent work and most of it was in good shape. The real problem was that thousands of years ago this canyon had been gouged out of the granite heart of the Sierra by massive glaciers and all the bedrock left had a surface of glacial polish. That means that if one of the animals stepped off the actual trail, it looked to him like he was stepping on good, solid rock. Instead, he ended up with his hooves on a rock surface that was slicker than snake snot. This scene played itself out a number of times that day, but most times the animals managed to scramble back onto the trail. Twice they didn't and those were our two big wrecks for the day.

First off, we were luckily at a spot where the trail dropped down pretty close to the river before starting to curve around and climb again. The trail swung around a point about 30 feet above the river and the trail was blasted into the rock at the place where it swung back away. As the trail ducked off to the left, there was a deceptively flat looking patch of smooth rock straight ahead. I guess it looked like the right place to go, because Wes's lead animal, Red, went that way and had just started to slip when Wes jerked him back onto the trail. Joel and his lead animal repeated the maneuver. Lisa's string of three black mules managed to get all of themselves out on the slick rock, and the end mule, Pete, went down. As Lisa leaped off her horse and frantically cut ropes to her mules, Pete went down and tumbled end over end down 30 feet of slick, steep rock and into the river. Her other two mules, Tony and Lloyd, freed of Pete's weight, managed to stay up on their feet. Nonetheless the rock was steep and slick enough that they skidded all the way down and also ended up in the river. Our only break was that the really deep part of the river was on the other side. So our downed mules were only in about two feet of water.

Pete was in real trouble. He was down in the water and his load was all busted up. He couldn't get up and his off hind hoof was jammed up under his back cinch. As he struggled to pull it free, several of the cinch strands jammed in between his hoof and his shoe. There was blood in the water but you couldn't see how bad he was hurt. Wes, who was in the lead, stayed with the stock on the trail. The rest of us bailed off our animals and slipped and slid down the rock into knee-deep icy water. We got to the mules as quick as we could. Joel got to Pete first, and Lisa went after the other two boys. Joel made sure Pete's head was out of the water, and then discovered the tangled foot. To miss being killed by Pete's flailing hooves, Joel went in along Pete's back and lay over the mule's belly to reach the trapped foot. Whipping out his knife, he managed to cut the cinch strands on both sides of the shoe and free Pete's hoof. Considerably less panicked now that he could move that leg, Pete stayed mostly quiet while Joel with some help from the old cook, managed to unpack and unsaddle him. Once the weight was off of him, he was able to struggle to his feet.

Lisa managed to get the other two mules back up to the trail without having to repack them. She then came back down and led Pete up to the trail while Joel and I dragged all his tack and load out of the water and up the rock to the trail. Joel and Lisa resaddled and repacked Pete's load and we were ready to hit the trail again. Poor old Pete was pretty scraped up and some of his duffle was damaged, but he was basically okay. Swinging up on Abby mule, I watched the cold river water run out of my boots while I thought about how lucky we had been. Looking back, if I had realized then how many more disasters awaited us on this trip, I would have sat right there and cried like a baby.

Working its way down the canyon, the trail climbed high on the canyon wall, dropped back down then climbed higher still. All this time the river was dropping away under us as it rushed downhill toward the west side of the Sierra. Eventually we reached The Devil's Washbowl. So that you can have a clear picture of how this next part went I guess I'd better describe this particular piece of canyon.

The whirlpool that gave the area its name was still about a mile downstream, but this part was tough enough. The walls were over 1,000 feet above us. They were pretty much slick rock like I told you about before. They came down pretty shear until you were about 80 feet above the river then leveled out a little into a lip covered in jumbled talus. From there the walls dropped straight and slick to the slot that held the trapped, raging river. When nature squeezes a river into a narrow slot like that, it picks up speed and roars like an enraged animal. Obviously, anything that went into the water at this point had no chance of surviving. We were working across the lower part of the face when the trail took a set of short switchbacks down the slick rock to the lip over the river. We should have been loose herding, but we weren't. I guess that was a good deal because Queen, the only loose animal, got confused and cut one of the switchbacks. Spotting the trail below her she tried to climb down to it, but began to slide on the slick rock. Picking up speed but still on her feet, she headed right for the edge of the drop-off. The broken rock on the edge of the trail tripped her and she dropped neatly onto the trail.

So she wasn't yet in the river's deadly churning waters, but she was in a pretty precarious situation. From her performance up in Dusy Basin we figured she wasn't just going to jump right back to her feet. So Wes and Lisa took care of the rest of the stock while Joel and I took a shot at rescuing Queen. We needed to get her up in one swift, sure motion. If she struggled or stumbled, it was less than five feet from where she was lying to the edge of the drop-off. If she got off the trail or fell again, we would have no real chance of saving her. First we took everything off of her except her halter and rope. To make it so that her head and front feet were downhill from her body and on the trail, Joel took her by the head and spun her 180' like he was playing spin the bottle with a thousand pounds of mule. Damn, that fellow is strong. Joel stretched her forefeet out in front of her, the position that makes it easiest for a mule to get up, and we were ready to try for that one smooth jump to her feet. Yeah, sure. Joel heaved on the lead rope and I yelled and popped her in the butt with a mule chain. She just lay there with a hopeless look on her face. She had given up, but Joel hadn't. We tried again. Same result.

I was just standing there wondering what the hell we were going to do now, when Joel walked over and climbed on Queen's back. Letting out a cowboy yell, he jabbed his spurs in her sides and she leaped to her feet. As she surged upward, he slid neatly off her back, and there they were, standing side-by-side, safe on the trail. In all my years in the Eastern Sierra I had only ever seen this trick tried once before. That was on a down cow in a cattle drive on Olancha Pass, and the kid that did it missed the "getting off" part. That rank old cow took him for a fast ride, and then threw his ass right in the rocks. Anyway, Joel and Old Queen were just fine and we went to repacking her right off. Pretty soon we were back on the move, but I must admit it was getting to be a pretty long day.

Onward, down the Middle Fork of the Kings River. As we lost altitude, it started to warm right up. In fact, it wasn't too much longer till I noticed that my soggy boots were getting just about dry. It was still a long way to Simpson Meadow. We finally dropped down off the high side of the canyon as the bottom of it began to flatten and spread out. And then we came to Cartridge

Creek. High above us we could see the water working its way down to join the Kings. Crossing the creek should have been a cinch since there was a nice wide bridge. Well, the guys that built this bridge probably didn't know much about big mules carrying big loads. Also several of our mules were young and green and had never seen a bridge except for the two they had crossed the day before in LeConte. Wes started across with two animals. Red had a fairly narrow grain load and made it. Cootie, a big red mule who was green as grass and carrying a large load, caught her load on the end of the bridge railing. She pulled back and dragged Red back off the bridge with her. We separated them and got Red across. When I tried to hand lead Cootie, her load caught again, and we realized that the angle where the trail met the bridge was too tight for an animal carrying a large load. While I quieted Cootie, Joel got the bow saw off the top of another load and just sawed off the end of the bridge railing flush with the upright. Then we were all ready to cross the bridge-- except for one little thing. While we were busy altering the bridge, my mule, Abby had headed off aways. After I got her back, Joel's entire string decided that they wanted to see what the lower canyon looked like from the wrong side of Cartridge Creek. After a while we all got headed in the right direction and rode on to Simpson Meadow.

We finally made it to the meadow just as the sun was getting ready to set. It was one of the prettiest places I'd ever been. Our hiker guests had beaten us there by several hours, had a campsite picked out, and even had a campfire going. They had gotten a good look at the trail that day and were feelin' a bit sorry for us. Luckily, the dinner that night was pork chops and pilaf, the easiest dinner on our menu. So it wasn't too long before everyone was unpacked, fed and settled around the campfire. Everyone was tired enough to head for bed fairly early. It was at this point, when it was just the crew left around the campfire, that we started talking about how we might be feeling just a tad resentful toward the boss for sending us on this trip. Thank God tomorrow was a layover day.

What can I say about Simpson Meadow? It's pretty big for the middle Sierra. It's covered in grass high as a horse's belly and surrounded by big ol' cottonwoods. The raging river from up canyon has gentled into a wide quiet stream riffling crystal clear over beds of rounded rocks. The water is mostly shallow enough to wade. However, where it swings in wide bends under the high cutbanks the pools are deep enough to swim in and full of nice fat trout. A layover day there was the next best thing to heaven.

The guests spent the day hiking, exploring, and fishing. Alden took some of them to look for the next day's river crossing. They also found some ancient Indian rock art. Doris sat in camp writing her journal in a tiny electronic notepad. The packers caught up on shoeing and repairing equipment damaged in the wrecks.

Cooks always use such days to cook the meals that take extra time. In this case it was Suisse chicken enchiladas made from scratch. You also go through all your food boxes and assess the condition of your food. On long trips with no resupply you continuously rearrange your menus to allow for the condition of the meat and produce. For the crew, a big part of such a day is the chance to swim, read, and especially nap. That evening around the campfire, we got a chance to go over our maps and plan the next few moves. Alden knew that country well, but wasn't real sure of what a pack animal could or couldn't do. That meant a lot of sharing of knowledge between the regular crew and our hiking guide. Also among the campfire stories that night was the question, "I wonder what became of the guy that lost the kayak paddle we saw yesterday along the river above Devil's Washbowl?"

The plan for the next three days sounded simple. We would cross the river and go about eight miles down canyon to a camp at the base of Blue Canyon Falls. We would layover there for a day so the guests could hike another couple of miles down canyon to the base of Tehipiti Dome, the highest dome in the Sierra. On the third day we would return up canyon to Simpson Meadow. What little we knew indicated that the campsite would be cramped and the graze would be sparse.

The next morning everything went well until we got out of camp. We were a little slow loading up because neither Lisa nor Wes could lift the 80 pound side loads alone. So they helped each other lift, and after I finished the kitchen clean up, I helped too. It was slow, but we got it done. Following instructions from Alden, we easily found the upstream river crossing and the start of the down canyon trail. It looked good and we only had about eight miles to travel so we thought we had it made. After the first couple of miles, the canyon narrowed and the walls got higher. We encountered frequent rock slides. The trail had been rerouted to scramble up and around each of these slides. Often such climbs were a couple of hundred feet up the side and then back down to the bottom of the canyon. Where the trail had been cleared, it became obvious that the trail crew had been allowing space for hikers, or maybe for small mules with light loads. It for sure wasn't designed for our big mules. Near the half way point Queen squeezed through a space where they had cut a large log. She caught her pack rope on the end of the log and it hung her up. She fell down and it messed up her load. We ended up unpacking her, getting her up and repacking all over again. I was beginning to think that having Queen added to your trip was about as much help as losing two good mules.

The farther we went, the lower, hotter and dustier it got. From the top of Bishop Pass to Tehipiti we had dropped around 6000 feet in elevation. The trail kept getting tighter and one of the young mules panicked every time she hit her pack against a tree or a rock. Finally, getting close to Blue Canyon Falls, we hit one last bad spot. It was an uphill scramble with two big, close set rocks on top. Beau hung his pack and got knocked down the hill. Joel got him up, unpacked him and hand led him between the rocks. Eventually, we had to unstring and unpack all the mules and lead them through separately. Then each mule had to be repacked on the other side of the rocks. Not far from there we came upon our hikers. They helped us get down the last quarter mile of trail, which involved chopping out a down tree, scrambling around a ravine, and other fun activities. I was lucky enough to have my mule Abby fall in a big hole that was hidden under pine needles. I came off. Abby managed to climb out and get back up. I got back on her not realizing that it was the last time I would do so for a quite awhile. Thus we at last came to our camp. It was small, tight, and dry. It was also way too close to the trail which we figured wouldn't matter as we hadn't seen one single stranger since we turned off the Muir trail three days ago. There was some argument about using this camp, but it all came to naught as there wasn't a decent camp within about eight miles of us.

Setting up camp quickly, Wes found a dead tree in a position where he was afraid that it might fall on the stock on the picket line. So he gave it a good hard tug to see if it was sturdy. It wasn't. It fell, but fortunately not on the horses. In keeping with our luck on the rest of this trip, it fell on Wes. The crew pulled it off him, dragged him to his bedroll, and medicated him up for the night. He was dented a little, but not seriously hurt.

It was comin' on to dark so I had to switch menus to come up with something that could be cooked quickly. The ham that was supposed to be baked closer to the end of the trip became ham slices and dinner was up in under an hour. The guests were getting to understand the kinds of days we were having and without being asked they all hauled in fire wood while Phil helped cook dinner and Alden did dishes. That was real nice. As I was getting ready to start the dinner fire, I made several observations that were not so nice. First off, there was very little in the way of stock feed there, just a few dry weeds and a deep mixture of oak leaves and pine needles. It was so dry that I cleared back a 10 foot circle around the stove. Before I lit the fire I noticed the smell of woodsmoke. There were no other campers nearby and the smell was a little more like a forest fire anyway. I assumed that that was what it was, but since I couldn't see the smoke I figured it was some distance away. It was pretty creepy to think about. We were trapped in a narrow canyon with walls two to three thousand feet high on both sides of it. Everything on the canyon floor was so hot and dry that one spark could have set the whole thing off. After cooking dinner we moved the stove and used the left over dinner coals as our campfire. We roasted a few marshmallows then put it out real soon.

The next day we laid over so our guests could hike down to see Tehipiti. They also fished, swam, did laundry, read and rested. It wasn't the best day of the trip. Even when you hiked down under the dome, you still didn't have a really good view of it because the trees and brush were thick and the canyon was so narrow. And of course the packers, especially Wes, were having a fit because the stock weren't getting much to eat. It was kinda pitiful watching them try to fill up on oak leaves and a few dry weeds. Joel and Lisa pushed them a mile or so down canyon in hopes of finding something better, but it was all the same. At least they had plenty of water at the river. The only good thing was that we knew that the next day we were going back up to Simpson Meadow where they could eat till they were as full as ticks.

That afternoon I had time enough to cook the dinner as planned. It was steaks and baked potatoes. Since it takes about two hours to wash, wrap, and bake those potatoes in the coals and another hour or so to do the rest, it was real nice to have the necessary time. It would have been nicer if we hadn't been at such a low elevation that the temperature was up around 100 degrees. Oh well, at least I got a swim in the river before I started.

During the night Joel tied up the horses, but left the mules out to forage if they could. The basic idea is that you control the loose stock by controlling the bell mare. Usually the mules will not leave the horses, and the horses who are mostly geldings won't leave the mare. In Tehipiti we learned that the operative word is "usually". When the crew wrangled in the morning, three old mules were gone. Queen was gone, which wasn't the worst possible problem, maybe even a relief. The real problem was that Pete and Abby were gone. Pete was an old but tough pack mule that we couldn't spare, and Abby was my personal riding animal. At first we were pretty confident that they were somewhere close looking for something to eat. There were no tracks down canyon so Wes took off wrangling up canyon on foot. I did the cooking breakfast, packing lunches, cleaning up and tearing down the kitchen thing. Joel and Lisa caught up, brushed, grained and saddled all the remaining stock. The guests ate, made lunches, packed up their duffel and took down their tents. Still no sign of Wes or the missing mules.

One rule in the packing business is that you never let your guests start out for the next camp until you're sure all the stock is in. Joel decided that this was an exception to that rule. Since the missing animals had gone the same way we were headed, the canyon was too narrow for them to turn off, and we had enough animals to move the camp if we packed heavy, it made sense to send the hikers on. Our hiking guide, Alden, would make sure they got safely to camp in Simpson. Joel told the hikers to give a message to Wes. Unless they met him in the first mile or so, he was to go on to Simpson and take the lost mules with him if he found them. Since Abby was one of the missing mules, I rode Wes's horse Huey. Being short a packer and having to put ten mule loads and some extra saddles on eight mules, it took until noon to finally get out of camp. Five minutes out of camp Huey stepped in the same hole that Abby had fallen in coming into camp two days before. He managed to scramble out and at least this time I didn't fall off.

Fifteen minutes after leaving camp we hit a bad spot in the trail. The trail was built up to go around a section of river debris that had been washed in jumbled piles and deep washouts around several enormous boulders that had fallen from the cliffs above us. The rocked up trail rose about eight feet into the air as it swung around a large overhanging rock. When we came down that way, the mules scraped their loads on that rock but then popped loose as they dropped below it. It didn't work the same way on the uphill. Joel got his big mare safely around it, but his string wasn't so lucky. His first mule, Rio, was big enough that he powered his load up around the point. The next mule, Aya, sorta hung out in space to get her load by. His last mule was Emma and she was green enough to get in real trouble. She hit her kitchen box load on the rock, tried to pull back, lost her balance, and went over the edge. Before either packer could get to them to cut ropes, her fall pulled the other two mules off with her. Though they only fell about eight feet, they all ended up in a pile, one on top of the other, upside down in a washout hole against a huge boulder. Looked real bad.

Joel and Lisa jumped into the mess and started cutting ropes to free the entangled mules. I was stuck with catching and tying all the other animals to try to keep them from adding to the disaster. They cut Rio's load free and he managed to struggle to his feet. With the remains of a busted pack saddle hanging off his right side, he took off down towards the river. Each time they pulled a kitchen box off a mule they had to drag it up to the trail so it wouldn't be in the way when the animal tried to get up. For those of you who have never seen one, a kitchen box is a big rectangular aluminum box with leather straps. When it's full as these boxes were, it weighs from 80 to 100 pounds. By the time they were done, they had dragged six of these boxes, top loads that included stoves and tables, extra saddles, and pack tarps and ropes for three animals out of the hole and up onto the trail. The last mule, Emma, was wedged upside down in the hole and I really doubted that they would manage to flip her over and get her out. But they did. They rolled her over, and we all held our breath while she struggled to get her footing in a hole full of tangled driftwood and sand. Finally up, she had to be led through the trees and rocks and back onto the trail about 50 feet from where she started.

Then they had to bring the animals one at a time to the trail to be repacked. Rio's saddle was broken beyond repair, but fortunately he was carrying one of the extra saddles off our three runaways. After getting everyone repacked, Joel led Rio up the trail where the big mule again powered his way around the overhanging rock. The little middle mule managed to dance her way around it one more time. Now all we needed to do was to get Emma around it. We were no more successful this time than the first time. After several tries, Joel unpacked her again and carried all her load up the trail past the rock. Then he led her past the rock and repacked her for the third time. That little wreck had cost us a total of three hours and Joel lost his good knife, but at least we were on our way again.

Since we were now five hours behind schedule and had about seven miles left to go, we loose herded the rest of the way. Finally hitting a bit of luck, we found that the narrow spot below Blue Canyon Falls where we had needed to unpack the animals on our trip down canyon was passable from this direction. After that we had minor problems like animals turning off the trail, and the green mule, Cootie, hanging her load on a tree every now and then, but we at least had hopes that we would make it to camp before full dark. We saw no sign of Wes, the lost animals, or the hikers. So we assumed that they were all ahead of us and doing okay. It was well into being dusk when we finally reached the river and found Wes signaling us toward the start of the hard-to-find crossing.

On the other side of the river we were relieved to find all our hikers safely waiting in camp for us. Less happily we realized that the missing mules were not in the meadow. As Joel and Lisa began unloading the mules I wondered why Wes hadn't followed us across the river, since it was shallow enough at this point to wade across. Just then I remembered him telling the guests at the campfire one night that when he had lived with the Mongol horsemen, he had learned that no real horseman ever put his feet in water that a horse might need to drink. If he was holding to that belief, he would still be stranded on the other side of the river. So Huey and I borrowed Joel's horse and went back for Wes. There he was, and gratefully he accepted a ride on Joel's big mare. Since he had hiked eight miles that day looking for my mule while I rode his horse, I thought going back for him was a pretty small payment.

As I said before, our three missing mules were not waiting for us in the meadow. I hated losing good old mules like Queen and Pete. But it broke my heart to lose Abby. I had owned her for ten years and covered over 7,000 miles on her back. She was my partner. The packers would look for them again tomorrow, but the chances were that they had backtracked over Devil's Washbowl. If they didn't get off on the slick rock or fall into the river, they could probably make it safely to LeConte Canyon. Above there they would have to trust to luck that someone had left the two drift gates open. If Queen didn't give out on the pass, they should be able to make it out to Rainbow's corrals at South Lake.

The mules weren't in the meadow, but what was there was a Park Service helicopter that was unloading supplies for a trail crew. Alden found out that it had landed in Simpson a numbers of times that day which might explain why our AWOL mules had left the meadow and gone on up canyon. A noisy metal bird dropping out of the sky will give even the quietest mule a desire to be elsewhere.

Now it was getting pretty dark and dinner wasn't even started yet. I had made so many menu changes that it was really getting hard figuring out a meal to cook for dinner. Proving that they were a great group of people, our guests all pitched in. Each person worked on one item. They made salad, vegetables, garlic bread, and dessert while I sliced the roast into steaks and bossed them around. In fact Evan, who swore he'd never cooked before, made the potatoes au gratin. Followed by a fair amount of alcohol and camaraderie around the campfire, it made for a pleasant end to a damn hard day. It was during this campfire that we started discussing doing Craig, the boss, some serious physical damage if any of us lived long enough to see him again.

The next day we laid over at Simpson for the second time. Joel and Lisa tracked the missing mules up canyon for quite a ways. When it became obvious that the mules had crossed into the nasty stuff above Devil's Washbowl a good 24 hours ahead of the trackers, Joel and Lisa rode back to camp. The runaways were now on their own and their survival was out of our hands. Our hopes were that they would go out over Bishop Pass. If they tried to just hang out in the high country, they would not last beyond the first big fall snow.

That night after a dinner of corned beef and cabbage, the fates must have realized that Lisa hadn't been hurt yet on this trip. So while we were doing dishes, she climbed under the work table to put a pan away. At that moment the table collapsed dropping the rest of the dishes, a forty pound kitchen box, and a lighted Coleman lantern on top of her. Surprisingly, nothing broke and Lisa wasn't hurt. Finally, some good luck!

Later, by the campfire we went over our move for the next day. We were going to be climbing three or four thousand feet up out of the canyon to an area below Granite Pass. It made us a little nervous to realize that the trail actually had a name in all the guide books. It was called the "Bitch Trail". Didn't sound like something to look forward to. At least there seemed to be a good horse camp there where we could stay.

The trail proved to be not too bad. It was a hard up hill for the hikers, but for stock it was a reasonable climb with no cliffs, rocks, holes, or other barriers to equine progress. Ironically, the trail gave us a far better view of Tehipiti Dome than when we were close to it. It also gave us a heart stopping view of a forest fire burning on the ridge directly above the place where we had camped three nights ago. The wind was moving the fire at an angle away from the canyon, but it was plain to see that in recent days burning logs had rolled down the hill and set off several spot fires near the cliff edge above where we had been camped. My belly clenched and rolled over when I thought how close we had come to being trapped there.

Reading all the guide books the night before, we had decided that we would camp where the trail crossed the creek below The Lake of the Fallen Moon. Here's the part where I got to be the guide. Yeah, I'm real good at it. I miscounted the creek and trail crossings, so that even when our guests found the correct camp, I thought they were wrong. This led to about an extra mile of hiking for the exhausted group. When I finally realized my mistake, I hung my head in shame and we all turned back to the camp. These really were good people, because none of them gave me the ragging I deserved.

It turned out to be a great camp; big flat area in the trees with a fire pit and old log table, nice little meadow for the animals, huge slabs of smooth rocks for sleeping in the sun, and enough of a creek for drinking water for animals and people. Like a lot of other nights on this trip, I cooked and cleaned up in the dark. Also like every other night since Tehipiti, I went to bed wondering how Abby was doing. Had she gone in the river, gotten trapped in the high country, or been stolen when she got nearer to civilization? The other mules were branded, but Abby was a slick. That means no brand and easy to steal.

The next morning was the beginning of our last layover day of this trip. It promised to be a truly beautiful day. While I was cooking breakfast, the packers brought in the stock, grained them, and then turned out some of them to graze. The plan was to let them out in groups all day long so they had enough feed in them to be tied up for the night. Joel's big mare got in a fight on the picket line. She and two of the geldings were trying to hog each other's grain. When Joel tried to break them up that nasty old girl drop kicked him through the goal posts of life. About another inch to the right and he and Lisa would never have had to worry about having kids. Wes and Lisa helped him to his bedroll where he lay moaning for a long time. Eventually, some packer pills (ibuprofen), some rest, and later some breakfast made him look like he just might live. Since he had been physically carrying the entire trip, I not only felt sorry for him but also knew we would be in real trouble if his injuries were serious. Even if they weren't, I bet he was really looking forward to the next day when he would get to be on horseback for eight to ten hours.

During that layover day, I went over my remaining supplies. We were in good shape for dinner, and I planned to make dumpster eggs for our last breakfast. That's where you take everything left over and scramble it into eggs. It can be anywhere from awful to great depending on what you have. We had lots of extra eggs, onions, sausage, cheese and bell peppers. It should make a whole lot of really tasty breakfast.

The guests took full advantage of our day of rest. They put up a shower, heated water and enjoyed a warm wash. The Campbells went off to the Lake of the Fallen Moon to try out their fishing skills. Alden and his wife found some wild blueberries in the meadow to pick. The crew spent some more time planning what kind of cruel damage we might inflict on our boss. Joel, feeling enough better to join in the conversation, pointed out that after tomorrow's long ride out to Cedar Grove we would be so glad to see that big truck waiting to haul us home, that we wouldn't be mad at anyone any more. Leave it to Joel to be sensible and reasonable. Kinda took all the fun out of our plan.

As the afternoon wore on, the Campbells returned with a whole bunch of pan sized trout which they wanted cooked for tomorrow's breakfast. Alden and his wife spent about three hours picking tiny little wild blueberries. It took that long to fill one coffee cup. They thought it would be great if I could make blueberry pancakes for tomorrow's breakfast. It was starting to sound like our last breakfast would be enough food for about thirty people. Ah, well, better too much than not enough.

The last day we climbed up to Granite Pass through a couple of real pretty little bench meadows. One of them even had a tiny cabin built over a century ago by a trapper named Shorty Lovelace. Shorty must have really deserved that name as his cabins were usually five feet by seven feet with a ridgepole only a little over five feet high. I had seen one before over near Colby Pass and it was so little that at first I thought it was an optical illusion. Once over the pass we crossed Granite Basin which is flat, green, and full of little glacial lakes. Then it was a 5,000 foot drop to Zumwalt Meadows and Cedar Grove. Lots of long dry switchbacks. At the end we would meet Gary McCoy with the big stock truck and my husband, LeRoy, with a crew cab truck and a three horse slant. The plan was that four of the guests had their cars waiting at Cedar Grove and would leave from there. The big truck would take Wes, Joel, Lisa and most of the stock. It would pull out right away. There was room for the crew to sleep in the cab so they would make it home that night. LeRoy and I would take three head of stock, the other four guests, and some of the equipment. We would haul out the next morning for the ten hour drive back to Bishop. All the way down, I kept wondering if anyone would have word of what had become of our lost mules. I never imagined that our own problems were far from over.

It took forever to get down off that pass. We didn't have any real problems. There were a few ground wasps, but no one got stung. There was a weird spot called Tent Meadow. It wasn't flat and it wasn't a meadow. It was about three acres of open brush land on a fairly steep side hill. Out in the middle was a large, almost white, granite boulder. It was the size and shape of an old wall tent. From far away on another hill, it must have looked like a green meadow with a tent in it, thus the name. We worked our way down out of the firs and lodgepoles into the pinions, sage and dust. Finally we came out of the canyon onto a set of long switchbacks above Zumwalt Meadow. Far below us I could see my truck and trailer. So I knew LeRoy was there and waiting for us. What I couldn't see was the big yellow semi and stock trailer that should also have been there. That didn't seem right. As we got closer, we could see a couple of fair sized trailers and a small stock truck. No way of knowing if they were waiting for us or not.

When we finally reached the parking lot, the first thing I saw was LeRoy's smiling face. Before I could say a word, he said, "Abby is home safe." Boy, could he read my mind. Apparently, the three AWOL mules had made it back to Rainbow in one and a half days. In fact, Abby caught a ride to my house with a truckload of animals being hauled to Horseshoe Meadows and beat me home by four days. That was the good news. The bad news was that the big truck wasn't coming.

The new plan was that the local packer would use those trailers I had seen to haul our crew, stock and equipment to Cedar Grove Pack Station where we would spend the night. The guests would take their cars and leave, or spend the night at the hotel. In the morning Wes, Joel, and Lisa would take their riding animals, all but three mules, their bedrolls, food, and duffel and head back into the mountains. They would go up Bubbs Creek and cross the crest at Kearsarge Pass coming out at Onion Valley in about a day and a half. Craig would meet them there and haul them the rest of the way home. LeRoy and I would take all the rest of the supplies and equipment, three mules, and the remaining four guests for the ten hour haul around the southern tip of the Sierra and back up the east side to Bishop. While we were sorting and loading all this stuff, there was a fair amount of grumbling from the crew. I remember saying that I was way too old to be putting up with this bull. I also remember mentioning that I had quit Reds Meadow over a similar incident.

So we got home okay despite a road that was so high and windy that it took us three hours to cover the first 70 miles. LeRoy swore some of the turns were so tight that he could read the license plate on the back of his own trailer. We returned the guests to their homes and cars in Bishop. Then we dropped the mules and equipment at Craig's house. Finally, we drove the hour back south to Lone Pine, getting home after dark. Long, long day.

The next day around noon I drove up to Onion Valley to make sure that my crew made it out all right. Darn it! They had had a great time just riding free across the Sierra. No big loads, no guests to take care of, and only a few head to lead. I had felt guilty and worried about them, but it seemed that they definitely got the best of the deal. Craig had already met them with the stock truck and some cold beers. Somewhere around this time we decided not to kill Craig after all. Musta been the beer.

When I started writing this story a few months back, it was still fall and I was thinking that maybe I had had enough of this packing stuff. Seems kinda funny, but now that it is spring I seem to be thinking about getting back into the mountains again. In fact, I talked to Craig on the phone a few days ago. I even went so far as to ask if he had a job for me this summer. Well, he mentioned that they could use my help following mustangs in the Pizona during May and early June. And maybe I could help with the horse drive. Later in June there was the packing school where he would definitely need me to train the new cooks and packers. July was booked a whole lot fuller than last year. And August was booked solid. It sounded a whole lot like my butt would be muleback from mid-May to mid-September. Seems like I'm not really ready to give up the packing life just yet.

CPSIA information can be obtained
at www.ICGtesting.com
Printed in the USA
BVHW040239210522
637574BV00002B/9